INSIGH

C000052164

DUBAI
StepbyStep

APA PUBLICATIONS

Part of the Langenscheidt Publishing Group

CONTENTS

ABOUT THIS BOOK

This *Step by Step Guide* has been produced by the editors of Insight Guides, whose books have set the standard for visual travel guides since 1970. With top-quality photography and authoritative recommendations, this guidebook brings you the very best of Dubai in a series of 15 tailor-made tours.

WALKS AND TOURS

The tours in the book provide something to suit all budgets, tastes and trip lengths. As well as covering Dubai's classic attractions, and there are many, the routes track lesser-known sights and up-and-coming areas; there are also excursions for those who want to extend their visit outside the city.

The tours embrace a range of interests, so whether you are an a modern architecture buff, a desert-lover, a culture-vulture, or want to hang out on the beach, you will find an option to suit.

We recommend that you read the whole of a tour before setting out. This should help you to familiarise yourself with the route and enable you to plan where to stop for refresh-

Above: breathtaking Dubai.

ments – options are reviewed in the 'Food and Drink' boxes, recognisable by the knife and fork sign, on most pages.

For our pick of the walks and tours by theme, consult Recommended Tours For... *(see pp.6–7).*

ORIENTATION

The tours are set in context by this introductory section, giving an overview of Dubai to set the scene, plus background information on food and drink, shopping, sport and beaches. A succinct history timeline in this chapter highlights the key events that have shaped Dubai over the centuries.

DIRECTORY

Also supporting the tours is a Directory chapter, comprising a user-friendly, clearly organised A-Z of practical information, our pick of where to stay while you are in the city and select restaurant listings; these eateries complement the more low-key cafés and restaurants that feature within the tours and offer a wider choice for evening dining.

The Author

Matt Jones trained as a journalist with the *South Wales Echo* before joining the Sharjah, UAE-based *Gulf Today* in 1996. A subsequent move into public relations in Dubai saw him handle PR for several international companies. Since 2003, he has been a freelance writer based at Dubai Media City. He was a member of the team behind *Insight Guide Oman and the UAE,* and his travel writing has appeared in publications, including the *Daily Telegraph, Sunday Telegraph, The South China Morning Post* and the *Japan Times.* He is also a columnist for the weekly *Khaleej Times Weekend* magazine in the UAE.

Margin Tips
Shopping tips, historical facts, handy hints and information on activities help visitors to make the most of their time in Dubai.

Feature Boxes
Notable topics are highlighted in special boxes.

Key Facts Box
This box gives details of the distance covered on the tour, plus an estimate of how long it should take. It also states where the walk/tour starts and finishes, and gives key travel information such as which days are best to do it as well as handy transport tips.

Footers
Those on the left-hand page give the itinerary name, plus, where relevant, a map reference; those on the right-hand page show the main attraction on the double page.

Food and Drink
Recommendations of where to stop for refreshment are given in these boxes. The numbers prior to each restaurant/café name link to references in the main text. On city maps, restaurants are plotted.

The $ signs at the end of each entry reflect the approximate cost of a two-course meal for two, with a glass of house wine, where alcohol is available. These should be seen as a guide only. Price ranges, also quoted on the inside back flap for easy reference, are as follows:

$$$$$	Dhs500 and above
$$$$	Dhs400–500
$$$	Dhs200–400
$$	Dhs100–200
$	Dhs100 and below

Route Map
Detailed cartography shows the itinerary clearly plotted with numbered dots. For more detailed mapping, see the pull-out map slotted inside the back cover.

MODERN ARCHITECTURE

In the last 20 years Dubai has altered beyond recognition, and it now has a truly 21st-century skyline (tour 1). It is also worth taking a look at Dubailand, a city in the making (tour 7).

RECOMMENDED TOURS FOR...

A DESERT EXPERIENCE

A visit to Dubai is not complete without a trip into the desert (tour 11) and if you fancy going further afield go to Hatta fort and springs in the Hajar Mountains (tour 12).

OFF THE BEATEN TRACK

A tour round the other emirates gives a flavour of Dubai before the oil boom (tours 13 and 14) and, of course, there are some lovely deserted beaches to discover here too (tour 14).

A TASTE OF ADVENTURE

An exciting way to see Dubai is to take to the skies in a helicopter (tour 5): a novel way to take in the striking architecture of the Burj Al Arab and The Palm Jumeirah.

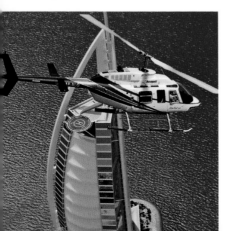

HIT THE BEACHES

Jumeira has some classy beach resorts (tour 3) but for some of the more off-the-beaten track beaches head out of Dubai to Fujairah (tour 14).

CULTURE-VULTURES

Despite its plethora of modern buildings Dubai has some wonderful historical enclaves such as Bastakiya (tour 1). Dubai's best heritage sights are covered in tour 4 or visit a mosque and enjoy a cultural lunch (tour 10).

DUBAI FROM THE WATER

Abras are a common way to get around Dubai and for visitors a delightful way to take in views of the dramatic skyline along the Creek (tour 1); for an alternative watery experience take a trip on a sightseeing dhow (tour 6).

SHOPPING IN SOUKS

For a local shopping experience try shopping in the traditional souks of Deira (tour 2) for vegetables, fish and even gold. You will have to learn the art of bartering, though.

WILDLIFE LOVERS

Either go birdwatching in Dubai itself (tour 8) or try your luck at spotting the rare Arabian leopard in the wilds of the Hajar Mountains (tour 12).

SPORTY TYPES

Nad Al Sheba racecourse and the camel racetrack give a view of life in the fast lane (tour 3). You can attend a race night there, too (tour 9).

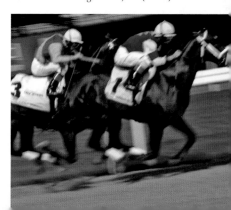

ORIENTATION

An overview of Dubai's geography, customs and culture, plus illuminating background information on food and drink, shopping, sport, beaches and history.

OVERVIEW

Dubai is a modern Arabian metropolis, a regional hub for business and leisure and an international crossroads. This overview of its geography, culture and people provides an ideal complement to the itineraries.

Above: traditional *dhow*; Burj Al Arab, viewed from above; 4x4 in the desert.

Dubai's rise from unknown to household name confirms the adage that in the world of celebrity it can take 20 years to become an overnight success. In the late 1980s, few people outside the oil industry would have found this former fishing and pearling village on a map. It has now become a celebrity destination, with, among others, film star George Clooney making his movie *Syriana* here, Morgan Freeman being a regular at its annual film festival, and Brad Pitt and Angelina Jolie having vacationed here.

Reviews

The reviews in the international media confirm Dubai's spreading fame. *National Geographic* described it as 'The world's hottest property' in a January 2007 cover story; 'Las Vegas is a sputtering 20-watt bulb compared with this fire in the desert,' said *Vanity Fair* in a glossy 20-page spread; Fox News proclaimed it 'The hippest city in the world'; and Britain's *Daily Telegraph* called it 'Wonderful... Sunny, civilised, sophisticated'.

Variously reported as the most popular Middle East destination after Egypt and the fastest-growing tourism destination in the world, glamorous, cosmopolitan and vibrant, Dubai is truly sensational.

URBAN AREAS

Dubai is the second city (after Abu Dhabi) of the United Arab Emirates (UAE), a federation of seven sheikhdoms on the Arabian (Persian) Gulf. The city is contained by the sea to the west, the emirate of Sharjah to the north-east, and by desert to the south and east. However, this vast sandy expanse has not limited the city's boundaries: oil wealth, bulldozers and seawater-desalination plants have all played a part in taming the desert. Add land reclamation for the breath-taking The Palm and The World island projects, and Dubai sprawls far beyond the confines of its original site.

The Hubs

The traditional centre of the city is the Creek, where the original communities of Shindagha, Bur Dubai and Deira developed, yet the city has expanded along the Jumeira coast and the parallel Sheikh Zayed Road, which leads south-west.

An area known as 'New Dubai' is springing up between Al Barsha and Jebel Ali, where the new Dubai World Central airport will be located. Inland lies Dubailand (see p.64), a massive leisure and residential development with several theme parks planned.

Did You Know?
In Arabic names, 'Bin' and 'Ibn' both mean 'son of': Mohammed Bin Rashid is Mohammed son of Rashid. 'Bint' is 'daughter of'.

THE DESERT

Dubai is the capital of the emirate of Dubai, which covers some 3,900 sq km (1,506 miles). While the city itself is flat, the topography inland consists of rolling dunes and the foothills of the Hajar Mountains. Climbing to a peak of 2,000m (6,560ft), the Hajar range separates Dubai from Oman – just over an hour's drive from the city – and the Arabian Sea. The desert is a playground for residents with four-wheel-drive vehicles, motorbikes and quads, but it is large enough not to be adversely affected; for visitors, an off-road adventure with a licensed tour operator is a must. The UAE's largest desert conservation reserve centres around the luxury Al Maha Resort, where rare Arabian oryx roam free.

CLIMATE

Summers in Dubai are hot and humid. From May to September daytime temperatures rarely fall below 40°C (104°F), with humidity up to 90 per cent. From October to April, the weather resembles an extremely good European summer,

Above from far left: the Emirates Towers dominate the Jumeira skyline; interior of the dome of Ibn Battuta Mall, the largest themed shopping mall in the Middle East; local man; the desert.

Below: Arab men having lunch together.

Above from left: high-rise city skyline; camel; palm tree; spectacular interior of the Burj Al Arab.

Below: the more traditional side of Dubai.

with temperatures hovering around 30°C (mid-80s°F) and with little or no humidity. Evenings can feel chilly in January and February, when sweaters may be required.

Rainfall
Annual rainfall is minimal (an average of 42mm/1.5in), but downpours can occur between November and March; when it rains, it pours, so if you plan to explore a *wadi* (dry river bed), check that it is not raining in the mountains, otherwise you could be caught in a flood. Inland, Hatta is a cool retreat from the more humid coast.

WHEN TO GO

November to April is when the climate is at its best. It is then that Dubai's lively sports and social scenes come to life, with open-air concerts by chart-toppers and touring productions of major Broadway and West End shows, such as *Chicago*, *Mamma Mia!* and Cirque du Soleil's *Quidam*. However, before you book, it is advisable to check when the holy month of Ramadan falls, as there will be restrictions on music and nightlife.

POPULATION

The population of Dubai was close to 1.5 million in 2008, but it is possible to visit the city and meet very few Emirati nationals except for those at airport immigration, the post office and the tourist information counters in malls. While the population of the UAE has one of the highest growth rates in the Arab world, hitting five million recently, over 80 per cent of residents are expatriate workers, notably from Asia, the Levant and North Africa. However, when you do encounter local descendants of the noble Bedu tribespeople, fishermen and pearl merchants, you are likely to find them charming, and keen to go out of their way to help you.

The Bedouin

One of the oldest tribespeople in the world, the Bedu were once nomadic herdsmen, living off the products of their animals. Today, however, Bedu culture and lifestyle are under threat from the modernisation that oil wealth has brought to the Emirates.

National Dress

UAE national dress is worn in the workplace, at home and when out and about. The men's white, floor-length robe is known as the *kandoora* or *dish-dash*. The cloth headdress, which can be white or red-and-white check, is a *gutra,* secured by a stiff black cord known as an *agal*, with which their Bedu ancestors hobbled their camels' legs. Increasingly among young men baseball caps are replacing the *gutra* and *agal.*

The most visible items of women's clothing are the floor-length black cloak, the *abaya*, and headscarf, called a *sheyla*. Older women may be seen wearing the stiff gold and lacquer face mask known as a *burqa*, though this is becoming less common. Children often dress in Western-style clothes.

Multilingual Dubai

Given the number of different nationalities resident in Dubai – upwards of 180 – you are as likely to hear Hindi, Urdu, Malayalam and Tagalog as Arabic. While Arabic is the UAE's official language, English is widely spoken and used for everyday contact between the various groups.

Parks

If you have covered the essential sights and visited the souks and shop-ping malls but feel somehow feel cocooned from Dubai life, you might enjoy a change of pace at one of the city's parks. They are open from 8am until well after dark, will have one 'ladies-only' day each week and mostly have small entrance fees. Dubai's oldest (est. 1975) park, the 64-ha (158-acre) Safa Park (Sat–Thur 8am–11pm, Fri 8am–11.30pm) is a favourite with joggers and local youngsters drawn by its fair-ground attractions. It also has barbecue sites, courts for tennis, volleyball and basketball and a football pitch. Perhaps the best park within the city limits is Creekside Park (daily 8am–10.30pm), an expan-sive green area with over 280 botanical species. It hugs the Creek for the 2.6-km (1.6-mile) stretch between the Al Maktoum and Al Garhoud bridges and has pleasant views across the water to Dubai Creek Golf & Yacht Club; it also has an open-air amphitheatre and hosts spectacular laser and fireworks shows. A fun way to see the park is from the UAE's first cable car system, which rises 30m (98ft) high, and runs parallel to the Creek, within the park. Dubai's newest park is Zabeel Park, which covers 51ha (126 acres) of the city centre between Karama and Dubai World Trade Centre. It has a 4.3km (2.6 miles) jogging track and a pleasant boating lake.

FOOD AND DRINK

From simple Emirati dishes with lamb or fish to colourful Moroccan feasts, Dubai offers visitors the Arab world on a plate. But this cosmopolitan city is also a culinary melting pot that caters for diverse international tastes.

Above: Japengo Café; dates; Al Nafoorah.

Zero Tolerance
Dubai has a zero-tolerance approach to drink driving. The penalty for being found with the smallest amount of alcohol in your blood can be a month in jail, with more severe penalties for causing death through drink driving. The bottom line is that if you're going to drink alcohol, take a taxi.

Dubai's local eating-out guides bulge with details of an expanding number of restaurants serving authentic cuisine from all over the world. From alfresco Lebanese eateries to hip New Zealand-owned cafés and no-frills sushi bars with racks of Manga comics near the entrance and salarymen at the counter, Dubai offers rich pickings for tastebud tourists. It may be a Muslim society, but the city is also liberal enough in its attitudes to tolerate both pork and alcohol.

WORLD-CLASS CUISINE

For dedicated diners, whether carnivorous or vegetarian, Dubai has all the ingredients for memorable meals, from roadside vendors selling cheap but delicious *shawarmas* (meat cooked on a vertical spit and served with garlic paste in Arabic bread) to the most elegant fine dining in luxury hotels.

Given the amount of money in the emirate and the increasingly cosmopolitan nature of both its inhabitants and visitors, it is little surprise that Dubai has developed into a regional centre for world-class cuisine. In 2001 British celebrity chef Gordon Ramsay chose Dubai for Verre *(see p.118)*, his first restaurant outside the UK. Other celebrity restaurateurs include India's Sanjeev Kapoor, who has Khazana at

Al Nasr Leisureland *(see p.116)*, and Bollywood legend Asha Bhosle, who owns Asha's at Wafi City.

WHERE TO EAT

Dubai's best restaurants are located in hotels that are vibrant social centres for nationals, expatriates and visitors alike. Those that have a number of different food outlets and bars feel like mini-neighbourhoods through which you can stroll in air-conditioned comfort. And in contrast to the majority of 'high-street' and mall restaurants, all hotels are licensed to sell alcohol.

For a combination of excellent food and pitch-perfect ambience, consider the seafood restaurants Al Mahara *(see p.118)* at Burj Al Arab and Pierchic *(see p.120–1)* at Al Qasr, Zheng He's Chinese *(see p.121)* at Mina A'Salamand, the European restaurants Vu's *(see p.121)* at Emirates Towers and Spectrum On One *(see p.121)* at the Fairmont. If it's Arabic food you want, try the Lebanese Al Qasr *(see p.119)* at Dubai Marine Beach Resort (not to be confused with the hotel of the same name) or Emirates Towers' Al Nafoorah *(see p.119)*.

Outside the Hotels
Away from hotels, popular Lebanese chains such as Beirut, Automatic and

Al Safadi offer excellent value for money. Other popular eateries include the funky Dutch-owned More bistro in the Al Marooj complex off Sheikh Zayed Road (there's another one in Garhoud, *see p.118*) and The Lime Tree Café *(see p.48)* on Jumeira Road (also at Ibn Battuta Mall, Jebel Ali). For waterfront dining, choose The Boardwalk at Dubai Creek Golf & Yacht Club *(see p.40)* or any of the outlets overlooking the canals in the Madinat Jumeirah resort. The atmospheric Bastakiah Nights *(see p.116)* offers a mix of Iranian and Arabic food in a restored house in historic Bastakiya near Dubai Creek. If you simply need fuel after hours of sightseeing or shopping, every mall has at least one food court.

TIMING AND PAYMENT

Residents tend to dine late at night, so for a good atmosphere plan dinner from around 9pm. If you're heading for a hotel venue, book in advance. Wherever you eat, major credit and debit cards are widely accepted.

ARABIC CUISINE

In the main, for Arabic food read Lebanese. Mezze – small dishes and dips – are the Middle East's equivalent of tapas. Staple mezze scooped up with flat Arabic bread are: hummus (a chickpea paste with olive oil, garlic and lemon juice); tabbouleh (a herb salad with bulgar wheat); *fattoush* (a finely chopped tomato, cucumber and lettuce salad); *mutabel* (similar to hummus but

made with smoked eggplant); and falafel (fried chickpea patties). Mezze are usually followed by a main course such as grilled meat, but can be enjoyed as satisfying meals in themselves.

Regional Dishes

Emirati food derives from simple Bedu fare and consists mainly of fish, chicken and lamb served as kebabs or biriani-style with rice. *Matchbous* is spiced lamb with rice, *hareis* is slow-cooked wheat and lamb, and *fareed* is a meat-and-vegetable stew poured over thin bread. Flavourings include cumin, cardamom and coriander. Al Dahleez, at Al Boom Tourist Village, is the nearest Dubai has to an Emirati restaurant.

Desserts

Arabic desserts typically feature nuts, syrup and fresh cream. Popular puddings include *Umm Ali* ('Mother of Ali'), a bread-and-butter pudding with sultanas and coconut, topped with nuts, and *Kashta*, clotted cream topped with pistachio, pine seeds and honey.

DRINKS

Delicious fresh juices are available in Arabic restaurants. Traditional Arabian coffee *(kahwa)* is flavoured with cardamom and served in small, handleless cups. Thick Turkish coffee is more commonly served in restaurants. If you don't like your coffee sweet, ask for 'medium sweet' *(wasat)* or 'without sugar' *(bidoon sukkar)*. Arabic-style tea, also served sweet, is without milk and flavoured with cardamom or fresh mint.

Above from far left:
Fruit and Vegetable Souk; tea-seller; Deira Fish Souk; cocktails at the luxury Dusit Dubai hotel.

Ramadan Rules
Whatever your religion, it is illegal to eat in public in daylight during the holy month of Ramadan, when Muslims abstain from food and drink from sunrise to sunset. Some restaurants open for lunch but screen off their eating areas. Although pork and alcohol are not consumed by Muslims, most hotel restaurants use them as ingredients in certain dishes. These will be highlighted with a symbol on the menu.

SHOPPING

For many visitors, Dubai's various attractions – from the cultural to the rest-and-recreation variety – are mere sideshows to the main event: its shops. For dedicated shoppers, male and female, Dubai is the proverbial paradise.

Above: wide range of wares from Cartier to 'hubbly bubbly' pipes.

Selling Dubai
World-famous Dubai Duty Free has led the way in terms of promoting the city on the international stage, thanks to its sponsorship of snooker, tennis, horse-racing and power-boating. But selling Dubai goes hand in hand with trading in gold, perfumes and a whole lot more besides at Dubai International Airport. With record annual sales of $712 million in 2006, Dubai Duty Free is the third largest airport retailer in the world.

Thanks to its large waterfront souks in Bur Dubai and Deira, Dubai was known in history as the 'city of merchants' and it remains true to its nickname. It is estimated that by 2009 retail trade in shopping malls alone will account for 50 per cent of gross domestic product, compared to a negligible figure for oil, which has all but run out in the emirate. From market stalls to the bright interiors of Harvey Nichols and Saks Fifth Avenue, Dubai's modern merchants offer an amazing array of goods, many of which are tax-free.

SOUKS

The Main Souks
For bargains and a vibrant atmosphere, nothing beats the traditional souks, the most famous of which is Deira's Gold Souk. The nearby Spice Souk is dwindling in size due to competition from local hypermarkets, but across the Creek in Bur Dubai, it's business as usual for the textile merchants in the Old Souk. Naif Souk in Deira is off the beaten track, but worth checking out, if your focus is fabrics.

Other Souks
Further afield, Sharjah's Blue Souk is one of the best places to buy carpets from Iran and Pakistan and also has a

wide selection of 'antiques', including decorative *khanjar* daggers: short curved knives traditionally tucked into men's trousers at the waist.

The best time to shop at souks is in the morning and late afternoon to evening; they are closed in the early afternoon and Friday mornings.

MALLS

For air-conditioned comfort, convenient access and, in several cases, the wow factor, try Dubai's malls. All have gold and jewellery stores that may satisfy you in the unlikely event the Gold Souk does not. Most open 10am–10pm, and later during the holidays and Ramadan.

The Crème-de-la-Crème
One of the grandest is Mall of the Emirates, near Interchange 4 on Sheikh Zayed Road; it has a branch of the upmarket department store Harvey Nichols, a large Arabian Treasures section for souvenirs and carpets, and an indoor ski resort (Ski Dubai).

Deira City Centre, which also has an Arabian Treasures section for one-stop souvenir shopping, is a perennial favourite, but vying with Mall of the Emirates as Dubai's swankiest shopping destination are the stately Bur-Juman Centre, home to Saks Fifth

Avenue in Dubai, and the Egyptian-themed Wafi Mall, both on the Bur Dubai side of the Creek.

Smaller Malls

Lamcy Plaza, on the same side of the Creek, is a little more downmarket but has a remarkable replica of London's Tower Bridge in its atrium. In Jumeira, the Italian-style Mercato Mall is worth a visit, as is Ibn Battuta Mall, if you are near Jebel Ali. If you rate ambience over choice, visit the Arabian-themed Souk Madinat Jumeirah.

ON THE STREET

Dubai has few open-air 'high streets'. Deira's Al Riqqa Road is a pleasant avenue of boutiques, while the parallel Maktoum Road's boutiques include Gianni Versace, Dolce & Gabbana and Cartier. In Satwa, there are boutiques dotted along Al Dhiyafah Road.

Electronics, Textiles and Crafts

For electronic goods, head for Al Faheidi Road in Bur Dubai. The port end of Khalid Ibn Al Waleed Road (Bank Street) in Bur Dubai is the place for computers and software.

If you want colourful silks or textiles, check out the many small shops to the rear of Dubai Museum in Bur Dubai, while cheap clothes shops and tailors can be found in Karama.

For local artwork, visit the small galleries that have sprung up around the Majlis Gallery in Bastakiya and in the Al Quoz industrial area off Sheikh Zayed Road. The Creative Art Centre

in Jumeira sells art, old maps of the region and other antiques. The open-air craft market at Dubai Marina is popular on the local Friday–Saturday weekend between October and April.

BARGAINING

Don't assume that because of Dubai's tax-free reputation, everything here is cheaper than elsewhere in the world. You can bargain for deals in the souks, but not in malls, unless you're in the Arabian souvenirs and carpets section – and note that you are more likely to get a large discount with cash. The trick is to disguise your interest in the item you really want, then offer half. How far upwards you go mostly depends on your cunning and the seller's guile.

Shopping Frenzy

The annual Dubai Shopping Festival (DSF) was set up in 1996 to cement Dubai's longstanding popularity with tax-free shoppers. It spans December to February (as commercial in Dubai as it is in the West) and attracts over 3 million people.

Below: textiles at Al Barsha.

SPORT

Dubai has gained an international reputation for world-class sporting events, and visitors can watch the stars of golf, tennis, rugby, horse-racing and other major sports here at various times of the year.

Olympic Hopeful

The world's first purpose-built city for sport, Dubai Sports City, is a feature of the massive Dubailand development near Emirates Road. When completed in 2010, it will have several stadia, an Ernie Els golf course, a Butch Harmon golf school, a David Lloyd Tennis Academy, an ICC Global Cricket Academy and a Manchester United Soccer School. Locals hope it will one day host the Olympic Games.

Below: Nad Al Sheba racecourse.

Dubai is synonymous with world-class sport, and the roll of honour of sporting greats who have competed in the city is testament to the international importance of its events. The emirate has the world's richest horse race, the US$6 million Dubai World Cup, and the world's most financially lucrative marathon, with US$1 million prize money each January. In 2005, Dubai Duty Free also became one of the few organisers of tennis tournaments to offer equal prize money for men and women.

Dubai also has a thriving exhibition calendar: in 2006, tennis legends Bjorn Borg and John McEnroe played what was billed as their 'last-ever' match in the city (McEnroe won); veterans of Manchester United and Liverpool football clubs compete annually in a Masters tournament here; and even the US Harlem Globetrotters basketball team makes periodic visits.

HORSE RACING

The Dubai World Cup at Nad Al Sheba Racecourse *(see pp.42 and 68)* may be the world's richest horse race, but it's also the party of the year on the city's social calendar. Held during the last week of March, the 2,000-m (10-furlong) race attracts the world's best thoroughbreds, jockeys such as America's Jerry Bailey (a four-time winner) and the United Kingdom's Frankie Dettori, and crowds of up to 70,000. Admission to the public enclosure is free, but to fully enjoy the day, buy a badge to the International Village in advance (tel: 04 332 2277). Definitely one to dress up for.

GOLF

Dubai has several superb golf courses, including the Montgomerie at Emirates Hills, the Four Seasons' Al Badia course at Dubai Festival City, the Arabian Ranches' desert course and Dubai Creek Golf & Yacht Club. But the first is still the most famous: the Majlis at Emirates Golf Club, which is home to both the men's Dubai Desert Classic in February and the Dubai Ladies Masters in October, won in its inaugural year (2006) by the then-world number one Annika Sorenstam.

Woods, Els, Norman, Garcia, Montgomerie and Faldo…all have played the Majlis and all have gone on to design their own courses in Dubai. Woods' Al Ruwaya ('Serenity') course in Dubailand is a world first for his company Tiger Woods Design.

TENNIS

Since the Dubai Duty Free Men's Open was first staged in 1993, the greatest names of the men's circuit have played in Dubai, Roger Federer being the most successful, with four victories by 2007. In 2001, when the women's World Tennis Association (WTA) event was held back-to-back with the men's, the two tournaments became known as the Dubai Tennis Championships. This two-week festival of tennis in late February and March is almost a sell-out from January, so it is advisable book early to avoid disappointment at www.dubai tennischampionships.com.

RUGBY

The Dubai Rugby Sevens has achieved the legendary status long associated with its Hong Kong counterpart in the International Rugby Board (IRB) Sevens World Series. The three-day tournament at Dubai Exiles Rugby Club near Nad Al Sheba is contested by the world's best teams every December. Daily and season tickets are available at the gate. To keep up with new venue details and for more infoation, visit www.dubairugby7s.com.

CARS, BIKES AND BOATS

The UAE Desert Challenge, a FIA-sanctioned car and motorbike rally, takes place every November, mostly in the desert but with one stage in a city venue. On road, the F1-standard racetrack at Dubai Autodrome hosts various other international events through the year. On the water, the final rounds of the UIM Class One World Offshore powerboat championships take place off Le Meridien Al Mina Al Siyahi in late October/early November. The Dubai-based Victory team are local favourites.

Above from far left: buggies at the Montgomerie golf course; scoreboard at the Dubai Tennis Championships.

Home Fixtures

Swedish golfer Henrik Stenson didn't have far to travel with his trophy when won the Dubai Desert Classic in 2007; his home is in Emirates Hills, just a five-minute drive from Emirates Golf Club. Danish golfer Thomas Bjorn also lives in Dubai, while footballer David Beckham owns a villa on The Palm, Jumeirah. The city is also a winter base for Swiss tennis ace Roger Federer, who has a pad at Dubai Marina and practises on the courts of the luxury Al Qasr hotel when he's in town. Dubai is even home to the International Cricket Council (ICC), which moved to the city in 2005 after 96 years at Lord's cricket ground in London.

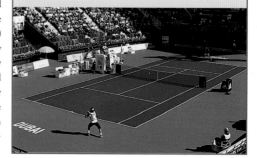

BEACHES

Dubai's beaches are clean, safe and seldom overcrowded. With the exception of Al Mamzar Beach Park (on the border with Sharjah), they are located southwest of the Creek, stretching for tens of kilometres between Port Rashid and Jebel Ali, beside the suburbs of Jumeira, Umm Suqeim and Al Sufouh.

Above: strolling along the beach; lifeguards on watch.

Statistics
Dubai's natural coastline is 72km (45 miles) long, but land reclamation projects are extending it by an incredible 1,500km (932 miles), which is longer than the natural coastline of the entire UAE.

Dubai's Arabian Gulf coastline, with its palm-fringed golden sands and azure waters, is one of the city's major draws. Indeed the outstanding quality of its beaches invites comparisons with some of the world's finest resorts.

Dubai does not have a picturesque, Mediterranean-style coast with sweeping bays and varying topography – here the Gulf coastline is straight and flat (if you want a mountain backdrop for your swim, head for the UAE's more rugged Arabian Sea coast); and the only elevated views are from hotel rooms and restaurants.

The coast isn't exactly unspoilt, either – Al Sufouh in particular is very developed, with new hotels and resorts at various stages of construction, both on the natural coastline and on the various land reclamation projects that are underway all the way to the emirate's boundary with Abu Dhabi.

But all that aside, most beaches have been carefully manicured, with trees, lawns or breakwaters added to enhance their appeal, and are swept by tractors first thing in the morning. They certainly deliver the rest and relaxation promised in tourist brochures in an environment that meets every holiday-maker's most basic requirements: sun, sand and sea.

KEY POINTS

Before you head off to the beach, there are just a few important things to note. There's a strong undertow and currents along the coast, even in the shallows, and, unfortunately, drownings are not uncommon, so beware. Always swim within sight of a lifeguard and never when the red flag is flying. One option is to save the beach for basking and ball games and opt to swim in a beach-side pool instead.

In terms of cultural considerations, restrictions are minimal – normal beachwear is acceptable, for example – but women should be aware that topless bathing is a strict no-no, and no one should walk around in bathing costumes away from the beach. Other considerations include special days for women and young children only, and, during Ramadan, changes in opening times of the beach parks and the absence of refreshments.

HOTEL BEACHES

All the hotels on the coast – including the Sheraton Jumeirah Beach, the Hilton Dubai Jumeirah, the Oasis Beach, the Ritz-Carlton Dubai, Le Meridien Jumeirah Beach, Le Meri-

dien Mina Seyahi, the Jumeirah Beach Hotel and the opulent One&Only Royal Mirage – have their own beaches. If you aren't a guest, most of these hotels will allow you to use their beach facilities on a daily basis at reasonable rates.

Even landlocked hotels such as Jumeirah Emirates Towers and the Metropolitan in Deira offer access to coastal resorts. One of the best of these, the Jumeirah Beach Club on Jumeirah Road, is a favourite weekend retreat for wealthy residents as well as visitors.

PUBLIC BEACHES

Alternatively, you can visit one of Dubai's public beaches, which, with their mix of nationalities and wide range of income groups, are more representative of the city. On weekends and public holidays these beaches and beach parks become focal points for popular events such as family barbecues and kite-flying festivals.

Access to Dubai's public beaches is unrestricted, although some charge nominal entrance fees. Beach parks are open from 8am until well after dark, but will have one 'ladies-only' day each week.

Most Popular Public Beaches

One of Dubai's most popular public beaches, and the closest to the city, is **Jumeira Beach Corniche**. The promenade at 'Moscow Beach', as it used to be known, stretches for 800m (875 yd) just off Jumeira Road next to Dubai Marine Beach Resort & Spa. Entrance is free and unlimited. Another popular public beach is next to Burj Al Arab (turn right where Al Thanya Street bisects Jumeira Road).

Al Mamzar Beach Park (8am–10.30pm, Thur and Fri 8am–11.30pm, Wed women only), located in the city's northern Hamriya district, has sheltered man-made bays and private chalets for hire on a daily basis.

Jumeira Beach Park (Sat–Thur 8am–11.30pm, Fri 8am–11pm; Sat women only), near the Jumeira Beach Club, is smaller but arguably has the most attractive stretch of palm-fringed sands in Dubai.

Above from far left: catching up on the news on Jumeira Open Beach; Jumeira Beach Park; Emiratis playing football on the beach; mother and daughter feeding the seagulls on a public beach in Jumeira.

Midnight Dips
If you go for a midnight dip you may see the luminescence of microscopic sea creatures around you – they give off a blue-green light when the water is disturbed.

Wild Wadi Water Park

Not a beach as such, Wild Wadi Water Park (Jumeira Beach Road; tel: 04-438 4444; daily Sept–Oct, Mar–May: 11am–7pm, Nov–Feb 11am–6pm, Jun–Aug: 11am–9pm; www.wildwadi.com) is a great place for seaside frolics. Situated next to the Jumeirah Beach Hotel, this 4.85-ha (12-acre) venue is themed around the Arabian Nights-style adventures of a shipwrecked seafarer called Juha, its 14 inter-connected rides run for 1.7km (1 mile). Highlights include the Jumeira Sceirah on which you drop 33m (108ft) and achieve speeds of up to 80kph (50mph).

HISTORY: KEY DATES

An introduction to the region, from fishing village to economic powerhouse, via the birth of the Babylonians, the dawn of Islam, the arrival of European powers and the rise of the Al Maktoum dynasty.

Above: the preserved ruins of an ancient settlement near Hatta and Fossil Rock; defensive watchtower in the walls of the Al Hosn Palace in Abu Dhabi.

National Day
The UAE's National Day holiday on 2 December begins four days of festivities celebrating the founding of the federation in 1971. At heritage venues in Dubai, look out for special exhibitions, cultural activities and performances of the traditional men's Ayyalah battle dance.

PRE-ISLAM

*c.***5000** BC	Stone Age settlements are established on the Arabian Gulf coast and in the Hajar Mountains.
2700–2000 BC	A Bronze Age settlement is established at Al Sufouh, Dubai.
1st century BC	An Iron Age village is established at Al Ghusais, Dubai.
4th century AD	Christianity arrives in Bet Mazunaye, an area corresponding to the modern UAE and northern Oman.
6th century	The Sassanids establish a trading post in Jumeira. Aramaic is the region's lingua franca.
*c.***632–5**	The Battle of Dibba marks the dawn of the Islamic era on the Arabian peninsula. Arabic replaces Aramaic.

EUROPEAN INTEREST

16th century	Portuguese imperialists recognise the Arabian coast's strategic importance en route to India's riches.
1580	The earliest surviving written reference to 'Dibei' is made by Venetian jeweller Gasparo Balbi.
1793	Dubai, a fishing and pearling village of 1,200 people, is a dependency of Abu Dhabi.
1822	A British treaty with Mohammed Bin Hazza is the first recognition on paper that Dubai is a separate entity to more powerful Abu Dhabi and Sharjah.
1833	Maktoum Bin Buti Al Maktoum and 800 members of the Bani Yas tribe arrive in Shindagha from Abu Dhabi. Maktoum rule.
1841	The Maktoums extend their influence across the creek, from Bur Dubai to Deira.
1853	The Perpetual Treaty of Maritime Truce between Britain and local sheikhs safeguards British sea trade with India. The region becomes known as the 'Trucial Coast'.
1894	Sheikh Maktoum Bin Hasher uses tax concessions to encourage foreign merchants to settle in Dubai.

| 1902 | Increased customs duties in the Persian port of Lingah prompt more foreign traders to migrate to Dubai's free-trade zone. |
| 1929 | Wall Street crash causes pearl prices to fall. The subsequent introduction of the Japanese cultured pearl sounds the industry's death knell and plunges Dubai into an economic depression. |

POST-WORLD WAR II

1951	Britain establishes the Trucial Oman Scouts to keep order and support oil exploration in the interior.
1958	Sheikh Rashid Bin Saeed Al Maktoum, the 'father of modern Dubai', becomes ruler.
1966	Oil is discovered in Dubai. Exports begin within three years.
1967	The population of Dubai reaches 59,000.
1971	The United Arab Emirates (UAE) is established with Abu Dhabi ruler Sheikh Zayed Bin Sultan Al Nahyan as President and Dubai's Sheikh Rashid as Vice President.
1983	Dubai Duty Free is established at Dubai International Airport.
1985	Dubai-based airline Emirates is established.

A NEW ERA

1990	Sheikh Rashid dies. He is succeeded by his son Sheikh Maktoum Bin Rashid Al Maktoum.
1994	Sheikh Maktoum's brother, Sheikh Mohammed Bin Rashid Al Maktoum, is made Crown Prince of Dubai.
1996	The Dubai Strategic Plan indicates that oil will run out by 2010; plans are made to diversify the economy. The Dubai World Cup, the world's richest horse race, is run for the first time at Nad Al Sheba Racecourse. Also the first Dubai Shopping Festival.
2001	Following a boom in tourism work begins on The Palm, Jumeirah, and The Palm, Jebel Ali, two man-made, palm-shaped islands.
2002	Leading property developers announce 100 per cent freehold ownership for non-nationals, unleashing a construction boom.
2004	Sheikh Zayed, the founder and President of the UAE, dies at the age of 86. His son Sheikh Khalifa becomes President.
2006	Sheikh Maktoum dies aged 62. His brother Sheikh Mohammed succeeds him as Vice President and Prime Minister of the UAE and Ruler of Dubai. Population of Dubai passes 1.4 million.
2007	Burj Dubai becomes the world's tallest building on 21 July, passing the 509m (1,670ft) record set by Taipei 101.

The Maktoums
The Maktoum family has ruled Dubai since 1833. The current ruler, Sheikh Mohammed Bin Rashid Al Maktoum, is also Vice President and Prime Minister of the UAE. It is the visionary Sheikh Mohammed who is credited for transforming Dubai from an oil-based economy to a centre for international commerce and global dialogue. Former US Secretary of State Madeleine Albright called Dubai a 'Davos with sand instead of snow'.

WALKS AND TOURS

BUR DUBAI

This leisurely walking tour begins with a look at Dubai's striking modern Creekside buildings, followed by visits to the historic wind-tower houses of Bastakiya, Al Fahidi Fort, Dubai's Old Souk and Sheikh Saeed Al Maktoum House. The tour concludes with a ride on an abra (water taxi).

DISTANCE 4.5km (3 miles)
TIME A full day
START Al Seef Abra Station, Bur Dubai
END Al Sabkha Abra Station, Deira
POINTS TO NOTE

Take a taxi to the starting point of this walking tour. Ask for Dubai Creek at Al Seef Road and get out at Al Seef Abra Station, across the water from the distinctive convex façade of the National Bank of Dubai Building.

Dubai has undergone drastic cosmetic surgery in the past 50 years. What was once a small fishing and trading community has become a commercial and leisure hub with towering concrete, metal-and-glass structures. A large proportion of the new prosperity has been reinvested on the wide crescent of Dubai Creek. Separating Deira from Bur Dubai, and cutting through the historic heart of a now sprawling metropolis, the Creek is much changed from the 1940s when British flying boats touched down here en route to Australia.

Bur Dubai Skyline

It is from the Bur Dubai side of the Creek that the two defining aspects of the city become most apparent: its modern skyline, which is kept youthful by enlightened city planners and the avant-garde skills of innovative architects, and the traditional. This tour will demonstrate that for all the city's fame, thanks to its tourist developments, international sporting events and shopping festival, and despite a fortune gained from oil revenues, it still retains a number of the characteristics of old, pre-oil Dubai, such as a cluster of wind-tower houses and the Hindu Shaif temple.

Below: loading a cargo dhow on Dubai Creek's Deira quayside.

AL SEEF ABRA STATION

The tour begins where Al Seef Road runs parallel to the Creek at **Al Seef Abra Station ❶**, from where you can catch water taxis across and along the Creek. Along the promenade here, in the gaps between the luxury yachts and charter vessels, fishermen of various nationalities still gather in the early morning to wait for *sheirii*, *safi*, *neiser* and catfish to bite. If you stop and chat to one of the fishermen, he might point out the various buildings along this stretch of the Creek.

The skyline here is extraordinarily modern. However, if you think it's impressive during the day, come back at dusk, when the lights are on and the fishermen have been joined by young couples and families.

Sights Across the Creek

Across the Creek, the tall building with the striking convex glass front that reflects the water and the passing river traffic is the **National Bank of Dubai**, designed by Carlos Ott and completed in the late 1990s. Notice how the glass is shaped like a sail – a Dubai motif found on numerous landmark buildings.

To the left of it is the **Sheraton Hotel**, one of the first on the Creek, and behind that stands the 'golf ball'-topped **Etisalat Tower**, the headquarters for Dubai's first telecommunications company. Further left, the

Above from far left: Bastakiya windtower; local man; architectural detail on a doorway; Dubai Creek, with cargo dhows and *abras* in view.

Above: *abra* captain with his boat; stairway in Bur Dubai.

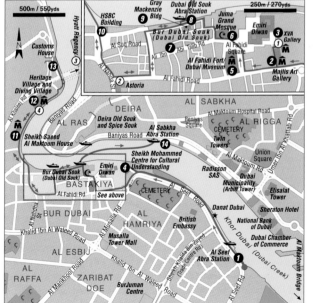

Gun Dancing

The ancient Bedouin rifle dance Al Youla is making a comeback in the UAE thanks to a popular competition initiated by Sheikh Mohammed in 2003 and shown on TV. The traditional dance involves the Yawil, or performer, spinning a weapon above his head as he moves to the music. Today, replica guns are used.

On the Water

The Danat Dubai (www.danatdubai cruises.com; tel: 04 351 1117), a modern sightseeing and dining boat, is anchored at the junction of Al Seef Road and Sheikh Khalifa Bin Zayed/ Trade Centre Road. The same company offers a more sedate ride aboard a wooden dhow. Bateaux Dubai (tel: 04 399 4994), the luxury dinner-cruise firm, is also based here *(see p.120).*

second building after the white Arbift Tower is **Dubai Municipality**, headquarters of the civic body that provides the emirate's public services. The **Radisson SAS Hotel Dubai Deira Creek**, formerly the InterContinental, stands next to it, while the identical oval towers further down comprise the **Twin Towers** shopping centre and office block.

To the right of the National Bank of Dubai is the blue glass wedge of the **Dubai Chamber of Commerce** building. Further right, the **Al Maktoum Bridge** is one of three bridges that cross the Creek (the other two are in the Garhoud area, further on) and, just visible behind that, the distinctive roof of the **Dubai Creek Golf & Yacht Club**, which recalls Sydney Opera House in miniature *(see p.41 for more details).*

Set between the Chamber of Commerce and the Maktoum Bridge are quays, around which are clustered dozens of wooden dhows, traditional fishing and cargo boats of the type that have sailed to Iran, India and East Africa since the days of Sindbad. The Arabian Gulf is out of sight, but roughly located westward.

ALONG THE CREEK

Now that you have got your bearings, it is time to move on. Follow the promenade on your left and head towards the mouth of the Creek for the rest of the day. It's about a 4.5-km (2.8-mile) walk, and there will be frequent stops for refreshments. You can find shade

under attractive Arabian-style canopies. More traditional wooden dhows and luxury yachts hug both sides of the Creek. If you look up Sheikh Khalifa Bin Zayed/Trade Centre Road, you will see the **BurJuman Centre** mall, which boasts Saks Fifth Avenue among many other stores.

British Embassy

At this point, the compound of the **British Embassy** is across the road to the left. (Britain has two embassies in the UAE – the other is in Abu Dhabi, the federal capital.) As you draw level with the Twin Towers, the Creek-side path widens into a small park and you can see the tall slender minaret of a mosque ahead. Rising from the Bastakiya district of old wind-tower houses, the minaret overlooks the grounds of the **Emiri Diwan**, or Ruler's Court, which now serves as Dubai's seat of government.

Deira Skyline

Across the Creek, the Deira skyline is lower now, more densely packed with older bank, office and apartment buildings. **Al Sabkha Abra Station**, the end point of the tour, can be seen in front of Emirates Bank International. You will now see – and hear – the crowded *abras* or water taxis in abundance as they put-put up and down this part of the Creek. There has been no development immediately to the left of Al Seef Road because there is a large cemetery there. This graveyard is thought to have once marked the edge of the old town.

BASTAKIYA

As you peel away from the Creek towards the wind-tower houses of **Bastakiya**, you enter a district with a rich history, dating back to the early 1900s, when fabric and pearl traders from Bastak in southern Iran settled in the area (hence the name). In building their homes of coral and limestone, they incorporated a feature common in their homeland – the wind-towers that have become synonymous with heritage and culture in the UAE. An early form of air conditioning, these four-sided open towers circulate cool breezes around the interior, while at the same time allowing hot air to rise and escape.

Historic District

The concentration of some 50 heritage buildings in Bastakiya gives a glimpse of what the streets of old Dubai would have looked like in the days before oil was discovered. Dubai Municipality embarked on a programme to restore these houses in 1996, using traditional materials and techniques.

The houses are impressive but fairly anonymous when viewed from the narrow lanes that criss-cross the quarter. It is only when you step through the decorative doorways and see the inner courtyards, rooms and balconies that you can appreciate the comfort these wealthy traders created for themselves in difficult climatic conditions. Especially impressive are the roofs and ceilings, constructed with hardwood from Zanzibar. Opportunities to venture inside abound, thanks to the numerous small appealing museums and art galleries that have been established in the district.

Majlis Art Gallery

One of the first Bastakiya homes opened to the public was the **Majlis Art Gallery ❷** (tel: 04 353 6233; Sat–Thur 9.30am–1.30pm and 4.30–8pm; all day in winter; free), on the edge of the quarter on Al Fahidi Road. The Majlis – named after the comfortable, cushioned meeting places under the old homes' wind-towers – was established in 1989 and showcases the work of a number of UAE-based artists, as

Above from far left: atmospheric alleyway in Bastakiya; Iranian *abra* captain waiting for customers; courtyard coffee shop at the XVA Gallery *(see p.30)*; Dubai Creekside viewed from Bur Dubai.

Below: the lanes of historic Bastakiya.

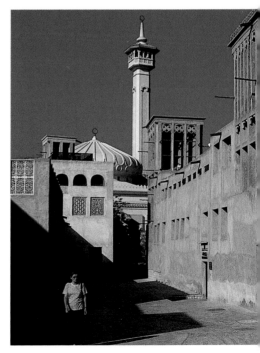

well as international ones with UAE ties. The gallery also sells traditional craft items, such as curved *khanjar* daggers (traditionally worn by UAE nationals until the 1970s and still worn by men in neighbouring Oman), goatskin water bags and jewellery.

XVA Gallery

In an alleyway behind the Majlis is the entrance to another arts venue, the **XVA Gallery ③** (tel: 04 353 5383; www.xva gallery.com; Sat–Thur 9am–9pm, also Fri in winter 9am–6pm; free), which has a lovely courtyard **coffee shop**, *see* ⑪①, and guest accommodation *(see*

Below: entrance to the Majlis Art Gallery.

p.113). The gallery puts on shows of contemporary work from the Middle East and across the subcontinent.

Sheikh Mohammed Centre

Another historic house is occupied by the **Sheikh Mohammed Centre for Cultural Understanding ④** (tel: 04 353 6666; Sat–Thur 9am–2pm; charge), which organises walking tours of the district, guided tours of Jumeira Mosque and visits to the homes of local people, to increase awareness between cultures. For more information, *see p.70*.

Dubai Museum

Head back to Al Fahidi Road, turn right and walk for about 10 minutes to Al Fahidi Square. **Dubai Museum ⑤** (tel: 04 353 1862; www.dubaitourism.ae; Sat–Thur 8.30am–8.30pm, Fri 2.30–8.30pm; charge) is housed within **Al Fahidi Fort**, which you can see to your right as you round the corner. Built in the late 18th century, the fort guarded the landward approach to the town. The boat in the centre of the square is a pearling *sambuk*, a reminder that Dubai's economy relied on trade long before oil. Inside the museum, give yourself time to absorb a history that dates back around 4,000 years. The displays explain how life was lived by traders and their families in coastal towns and desert oases over the centuries *(see p.57)*.

Juma Grand Mosque and Dubai Old Souk

The tour now jumps forward in time to the streets of modern Dubai.

Before lunch, pass, at the bottom of Al Fahidi Square, the **Juma Grand Mosque** ❻ (Al Mussalla Road; closed to non-Muslims; *see also p.57*), one of the oldest in Dubai; you can take a peek inside from the doorway, but, unless you are a Muslim, don't venture in.

At this point turn right down 54a Sikka towards Dubai **Old Souk** ❼ (Sat–Thur 8am–1pm, Fri 4–9pm). Most of the souk is devoted to textiles, of which there is an infinite variety; in other sections you can find handicrafts, carpets and silver carvings. Mornings are the best time to browse; note also that sales are sometimes held around holidays such as Eid and Diwali. Just before you reach the souk, take a few minutes to walk a short way up another narrow lane on the right, where stalls selling Indian icons and orange garlands mark the entrance to the Hindu **Shaif Temple**.

You might also take a little longer to walk beyond the souk entrance to the Creek. Notice how much busier the river traffic is here than at the start of the walk. There is, however, a fine view across the Creek to **Deira's Old Souk**, which features in tour 2 *(see p.34)*.

Dubai Old Souk Abra Station

The **Dubai Old Souk Abra Station** ❽, which links up with Al Sabkha Abra Station *(see p.33)*, is a hive of activity on most days, with any number of small boats jostling for custom at the wooden pontoons.

Slightly further on, the arched wooden doorways and narrow alleys

of the souk opposite Bur Dubai Abra Station (for the shorter hop to Deira Old Souk) have been well preserved.

Gray Mackenzie Building

Overlooking the *abra* station is the old, two-storey **Gray Mackenzie Building** ❾, constructed in 1932. This, the first purpose-built office building in Dubai, was the initial base for the city's British agencies and trade missions.

Pancho Villa's

Emerging from the far end of the souk, at 34 Street, take a left turn into an area that is known for its electronics goods shops. Head for **Pancho Villa's**, *see* ⑪②, in the Astoria Hotel. The sign will be visible as you turn right into Al Fahidi Street.

Above from far left:
Dubai Old Souk;
shoes off outside
Juma Grand Mosque.

Food and Drink 🍴

① XVA GALLERY

Bastakiya; tel: 04 353 5383; www.xvagallery.com; Sat–Thur 9am–9pm, Fri in winter 9am–6pm; $$
Delightful shaded café in the courtyard of a historic house that is now an art gallery. Menu offers healthy vegetarian fare.

② PANCHO VILLA'S

Astoria Hotel, Al Fahidi Street; tel: 04 353 2146; www.astamb. com; daily for lunch noon–3pm, closed Fri; $
Pancho's is a legendary watering hole and the Gulf's first Tex Mex restaurant. According to Pancho's lore, two American Flying Tiger pilots once phoned from New York to reserve a table. Journalists covering the Iran-Iraq war came here to relax, and, in 1987, *Time* magazine quoted a diner as saying that Pancho's had 'the best Mexican food west of San Diego.' Conversely, Bob Hepburn of the *Toronto Star* wrote, 'Pancho Villa's is a symbol of Dubai today: all glitter, all hustle, superficial.' With admirable mastery of the euphemism, this critique was paraphrased in the local press to read, 'the symbol of Dubai's lively, easy going and progressive lifestyle.' Both versions are displayed on the wall. The Dhs29 'Beer and a bite' lunch is excellent value for money. Chicken fajitas are a house speciality.

Above from left:
'hubbly bubbly' pipes;
dhows on the Creek.
Below: details, Sheikh
Saeed's House.

SHINDAGHA

After lunch head down Al Nahda Street towards the **HSBC building** ⑩ and the Shindagha portion of the Creek beyond it. Much like the streets at the start of this tour, this area has been pedestrianised. The view up river towards the *abra* stations and the jumble of Creekside buildings and minarets is stunning.

The dark, multi-storey monolith near the mouth of the Creek is the Hyatt Regency Hotel in Deira. Its **Focaccia** Mediterranean restaurant, *see* ⑪③, is something of a Dubai institution.

Sheikh Saeed Al Maktoum House

The next stop on the route, **Sheikh Saeed Al Maktoum House** ⑪ (tel: 04 393 7139; Sat–Thur 8am–8.30pm; Fri 3–9.30pm; charge), is in the immediate foreground. Dating from the late 1800s,

this rather modest palace, which once belonged to the eponymous former ruler (1912–58), is now a museum documenting the social, cultural, educational and religious history of the emirate. See rare photographs that chart the city's expansion from this strategic spot, and explore the various wind-towers, narrow staircases and rooms constructed around the large central courtyard.

Heritage and Diving Village

Located further towards the mouth of the Creek is the **Heritage Village and Diving Village** ⑫ (tel: 04 393 7151; Sat–Thur 8am–10pm, Fri 8–11am, 4–10pm; free). Featuring recreated dwellings, markets and displays, the combined 'villages' will reinforce impressions of old Dubai gained at Dubai Museum and Sheikh Saeed Al Maktoum House. The difference here is that

A Dynamic Dynasty

Dubai's growth from the late 1950s to the present is due mainly to Sheikh Rashid Bin Saeed Al Maktoum and his son Sheikh Mohammed. Sheikh Rashid, 'the Father of Dubai,' ruled from 1958 to 1990; before oil was discovered, he took out loans to build an infrastructure to ensure the city was well set up to exploit oil wealth when it came. He was often spotted inspecting construction work on Port Rashid, Jebel Ali Port and the Dubai World Trade Centre. When he died in 1990, his eldest son Sheikh Maktoum became ruler, but it was Sheikh Mohammed, younger son and Crown Prince, who was the new driving force behind the city's development, leading the push towards a more diversified economy. His brother died in 2006, and now 'Sheikh Mo' rules the emirate. He can often be seen driving around in his white Mercedes 4x4 with the number plate '1'.

Food and Drink 🍴

③ FOCACCIA

Hyatt Regency Hotel, Deira
Corniche; tel: 04 209 1234; daily
12.30–3pm, 7pm–midnight; $$
A Dubai favourite, this Mediterranean restaurant has a lovely laid-back vibe and wonderful sea views. Italian staples with a contemporary twist, and fresh seafood; regular theme nights.

④ KAN ZAMAN

Creekside, Shindagha; tel: 04 393 9913; daily 10am–1.30am; $
Meaning 'Once upon a time', this huge Arabic restaurant with outdoor seating has a pleasant creekside setting. Lebanese mezze, Turkish coffee and shisha ('hubbly bubbly' pipes) available.

you may get to see real people rather than mannequins re-enacting aspects of local life. You will also have the opportunity to spend your *dirhams* in the villages' handicraft shops or have a bite to eat at **Kan Zaman**, see ⑪④.

Customs House

If you have the energy to walk for another 15 minutes to the **Customs House** ⑬ at the mouth of the Creek, assuming it is not hazy, you will be rewarded with a view north along the coast to the neighbouring city and emirate of Sharjah. The starting point for the next tour *(see p.34)*, Deira's **Fish Souk**, is just across the Creek.

ABRA RIDE

Doubling back towards Bur Dubai, now head for the *abras*. Ignore the first *abra*

station, the Bur Dubai one, and head for the Dubai Old Souk Abra Station, which connects with **Al Sabkha Abra Station** ⑭. The 10-minute ride across the Creek during *abra* rush hour costs just one *dirham* per person but could well be one of the highlights of your visit to Dubai, as you find yourself sitting among regular commuters crossing this timeless water highway. An *abra* ride conveys an overwhelming sense of place and gives visitors an insight into the pace at which people live their lives here.

Once at our destination on the Deira side of the Creek, you will be able to look back on a panoramic view of the area the tour explored today. Refreshed by a fruit juice from the nearby stall, watch as the sun sinks over the rooftops, silhouetting Bur Dubai's evocative *Arabian Nights* skyline of wind-towers and minarets.

Abra Commuters

Around 15,000 commuters (mostly lower-paid workers) use these wooden water taxis to take them over the Creek every day. The boats were originally powered by oar, but now have rather more environmentally unfriendly diesel engines to propel them through the water. In terms of etiquette, note that boarding is to the left, alighting to the right.

Below: traditional hanging jars and dwelling at the Heritage Village, with a wind-tower behind.

DEIRA

Traders at Deira's various souks will try to part you from your dirhams during this leisurely day-long walking tour. Heritage buildings, the dhow quays and the greens of Dubai Creek Golf & Yacht Club are among the highlights in an itinerary that ends with cocktails at the Boardwalk.

Above from left:
Deira's waterfront; invitingly fresh produce at the Fruit-and-Vegetable Souk.

DISTANCE 11km (7 miles)
TIME A full day
START Fish Souk, near the Hyatt Regency
END Dubai Creek Golf & Yacht Club
POINTS TO NOTE

Take a taxi to the starting point of this tour. Ask for the Fish Souk in Deira, near the Hyatt Regency hotel. In the afternoon, you will need to take two more taxis, from Dubai Chamber of Commerce to Naif and from Naif to Dubai Creek Golf & Yacht Club. Each fare won't be more than Dhs20. Unless otherwise indicated, the souks are open Sat–Thur 9am–1pm, 4–10pm, Fri 4–10pm.

Below: at the Fish Souk.

While Western consumers are often amazed by Dubai's variety of modern air-conditioned malls, the city certainly has not turned its back on its famous souks. Most of the specialist markets are clustered in an area bordered roughly by the Arabian Gulf, the Creek and Al Sabkha Road in Deira. The souks are vibrant markets where you will see people in traditional dress among those shopping for fish, spices, halal meat and that other Dubai staple, gold.

FISH SOUK

The day starts at the **Fish Souk** ❶ on the Gulf side of Al Khaleej Road. Before venturing inside, take time to wander among the ice lorries parked to the right of the main building. The fish are kept here in iceboxes and either wheeled into the market by barrow-bearing porters or sold to bulk buyers such as restaurateurs. You'll be amazed at the variety of shapes and sizes of fish, and, here in the sun, you can also appreciate their often stunning colours. Red snappers, belt fish, up to 1.5-m (5-ft) long kingfish, sardines and baby sharks are among those weighed and tossed into barrows or flat-bed trucks.

Towards the Souk

Walk parallel to the open-sided main building towards the clusters of people at the far end. Shopping is viewed as a social activity in Dubai, and the appeal of this souk, as with the others you will visit today, lies not only in what is being sold, but in who is doing the buying. Notice the old-timers chatting on the wooden benches, dressed in *dishdasha* (men's ankle-length robe, also known as a *kandoura* or *jalabiya*) and waving walking sticks to emphasise their point; and those who rub their prayer beads before taking the bait and joining in the lively, good-natured general debate.

Inside the Souk

In the market proper, walk between the trays of fish towards the sound of chop-ping at the top left of the hall. Here, buyers can have their fish descaled, fil-leted and diced by an army of knife-wielding workers in blue overalls.

MEAT AND VEG SOUKS

Next to this section – but definitely not for those of a squeamish disposition – is the smaller **Meat Souk ❷**, where skinned goats (the carcasses come com-plete with tails), lambs (without tails) and cows hang. Somewhat easier on both the nose and the eye is the **Fruit-and-Vegetable Souk ❸** in the next hall.

GOLD SOUK

After leaving the market halls on the Hyatt Regency side, cross the car park

Above: men outside the Fish Souk.

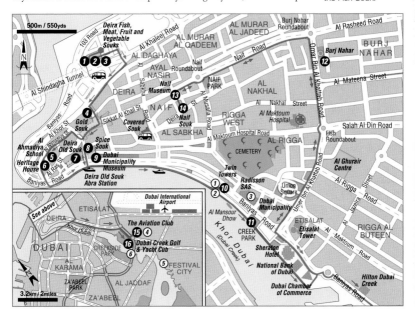

Gold Jewellery

Dubai is considered to be among the cheapest places to buy gold in the world. Unless complex jewellery-making is involved, items can be bought at the daily gold price, displayed at the entrance to the Gold Souk. Surprisingly, workmanship is not a factor in price. Gold is an essential component of a bride's dowry: most expect to receive a full complement of gold jewellery, including headdress, rings, necklaces and bracelets; these pieces will often be specially commissioned.

Bargaining

If you are interested in buying something at the Gold Souk, do not reveal your full interest to the seller. Start your offer low – at around half the amount you estimate you would finally like to spend.

and head for the footbridge that crosses the busy Al Khaleej Road. Passing now into the Al Ras district of Deira, turn right off the bridge. Ignore the Gold Land building and continue for 450m/yds along Al Khor Street. Turn left on 45 Street and you will see, 90m/yds ahead, a wooden entrance to the covered **Gold Souk** ❹ (Sat–Thur 7am–noon, 5–7pm, Fri 5–7pm).

The main part of this famous souk runs along Sikkat Al Khail Street, along which it is worth spending the next hour or so trying to resist Dubai's 14-, 18-, 22- and 24-carat sirens. The area's antiques shops are definitely worth exploring, and you can quench your thirst with a fruit juice here, too.

HERITAGE SIGHTS

Turn right out of the Gold Souk onto Old Baladiya Street and follow it around onto Al Ahmadiya Street. You now have the opportunity to visit two cultural gems – Al Ahmadiya School and Heritage House. Like Bastakiya and Sheikh Saeed Al Maktoum House in the first walk, these two recently restored buildings paint a fascinating portrait of life in old Dubai.

Al Ahmadiya School

Al Ahmadiya School ❺ (Al Ahmadiya Street; tel: 04 226 0286; 8am–7.30pm, Fri 2.30–7.30pm; free), the first in Dubai, was established in 1912. This is where Dubai's future rulers received their education. For more information on the school's history, *see p.55*.

Like most of the buildings from that era, the decorative doorway opens into a courtyard, or *al housh*, surrounded by verandas *(liwan)* and various rooms. The courtyard was the place where children once listened to school messages, did their exercises, had their breaks, recited poetry and took part in annual events.

Moving anticlockwise through the ground floor, you will see the water-drinking room, the small kitchen, exhibitions on the development of education in the UAE and the school's history, the library, a display of social activities, and a traditional classroom. There are more classrooms upstairs.

Heritage House

Next door is the **Heritage House** ❻ (Al Khor Street; tel: 04 226 0286; 8am–7.30pm, Fri 2.30–7.30pm; free), which from 1910 was the residence of Ahmad bin Dalmouk, the local pearl merchant who founded Almadiya School (and after whom it was named). The building dates back to 1890 and has changed hands a number of times, undergoing various extensions in the process. It was bought by Dubai Municipality in 1993 and has been renovated with the use of traditional materials and methods. The house is now preserved as a reminder of the pre-oil 1940–60 era.

DEIRA OLD SOUK

Returning to the souks, a five-minute walk along Al Ahmadiya Street brings you to Baniyas Road and the Creek,

(see p.28). The view of the bustling waterway and skyline is superb. A short walk up the Creek is **Deira Old Souk Abra Station**. Here, cross the road and enter the warren of lanes and alleyways at the bottom of Old Baladiya Street that make up **Deira Old Souk ❼**, an interesting place to explore for an hour or so. Notice how shops selling similar items are grouped together: rice and pulses, textiles and clothing, stationery and so forth.

Within the Old Souk, the **Spice Souk ❽**, where stallholders display sacks of fragrant nutmeg, frankincense, saffron and cardamom, is shrinking due to fierce competition from hypermarkets such as the French chain Carrefour. It occupies the alleys behind **Dubai Municipality Museum ❾** (tel:

04 225 3312; Sat–Thur 8.30am–8.30pm, Fri 4–8.30pm; free), the first-floor balcony of which makes an interesting viewing platform. Inside the museum, the civic history of Dubai is illustrated with important documents and rare photographs.

DHOW MOORINGS

Cross Baniyas Road, head back to Deira Old Souk Abra Station, then continue walking along the quayside in the direction of the blue-glass **Twin Towers ❿**. Now you will get a close look at the dhows, wooden cargo boats you see plying back and forth along the Creek. Their crew members might be busy loading industrial cargo such as vacuum cleaners and car parts to transport to

Above: Burj Nahar;
Deira mosque.

other Gulf states, India, Pakistan and East Africa, or they might be resting on deck or performing public ablutions in the peculiar boxes strapped to the stern – don't look too closely, just in case.

Along the Creek

About half way to the Twin Towers, the Creek widens at **Al Sabkha Abra Station**. In the distance, beyond the Al Maktoum Bridge, is today's final destination, the **Dubai Creek Golf & Yacht Club** *(see p.41)*. At this part of the Creek the best place to eat is on the balcony of the Twin Towers' third-floor food court, where you can look back on the route taken. The Iranian **Danial** restaurant, *see* ⑪①, and the cheap and cheerful **Apple Café and Restaurant**, *see* ⑪②, both of which

have balconies, are two options. Alternatively, you can continue along Baniyas Road to the **Radisson SAS Hotel Dubai Deira Creek** (formerly the InterContinental Hotel & Plaza), where there's a choice of food outlets including **La Moda**, *see* ⑪③.

CREEK PARK

After lunch cross Baniyas Road to the **Creek**. The Radisson SAS's *Al Mansour Dhow*, which offers dinner cruises for residents and non-residents alike, is moored here. From here, the Creek-side car park gives way to the small but pleasant **Creek Park** ⑪.

To the left, forming a backdrop to the park's centrepiece statue of a camel, is the Dubai Municipality building. Ahead, beyond the lawns, admire the impressive skyline that includes among its skyscrapers the Sheraton Hotel, the landmark National Bank of Dubai building and the Etisalat Tower, topped by a distinctive sphere.

Sightseeing Dhows

For the next 300m/yds or so you will see a variety of sightseeing dhows moored to the right. All have sailing times, prices and contact numbers displayed on boards near the gangways. About 20 minutes' walk from the Twin Towers you will pass in front of the National Bank of Dubai building and the three-sided Dubai Chamber of Commerce.

You can see commerce in action at a series of crowded dhow quays that point like fingers into the Creek. If you want to see more of the activity associated

Food and Drink 🍴

① **DANIAL**
3rd Floor, Twin Towers, Baniyas Road; tel: 04 227 7669; open 12.30–5pm and 7pm–12.30am; $
Iranian restaurant serving good-value buffet meals from 12.30pm. Enjoy the Creek view from the balcony during the cooler months.

② **APPLE CAFÉ AND RESTAURANT**
Twin Towers Shopping Centre, next to Radisson SAS Hotel Deira Creek, Baniyas Road; tel: 04 227 4446; open daily 8am–midnight; $–$$
Informal eating place serving Persian cuisine. It is popular with young locals who smoke sheishas on the terrace overlooking the Creek. The hot and cold Lebanese buffet is good value at Dhs30 per person.

③ **LA MODA**
Radisson SAS Hotel Dubai Deira Creek, Baniyas Road; tel: 04 205 7444; www.deiracreek.dubai.radissonsas.com; lunch 12.30–3pm; $$$
Ultra-stylish, contemporary Italian restaurant in a five-star hotel. The seafood risotto is a favourite.

with these elegant timber vessels, wander out to the tip of quays 2 and 3, where you will get yet another view of Dubai's skyline. Off to the right stands the Hilton Dubai Creek, designed by Carlos Ott, which houses UK celebrity chef Gordon Ramsay's **Verre** restaurant *(see p.118)*.

BURJ NAHAR

Now head to the Baniyas Road side of the Chamber of Commerce, and take a taxi to **Burj Nahar** ⑫, near Burj Nahar roundabout, which lies inland between the Creek and the Arabian Gulf.

In modern Dubai, *burj*, which means 'tower' in Arabic, is more commonly associated with steel-and-glass skyscrapers (think Burj Al Arab, *see p.50*, or Burj Dubai, *see p.45*), but this is an original *burj*, a round defensive watchtower built in 1870 with the simple materials available at that time to defend the coastal settlement from attack from the north.

Restored in 1992, Burj Nahar is located in a small park near the intersection of Naif Road and Omar Bin Al Khattab Road, which is your taxi's best route from the Creek. Along the way you will pass one of the main stations for the new Dubai Metro light railway in Union Square, off to your left; the **Al Ghurair Centre**, which was Dubai's first modern mall when it opened in 1981, to your right; and the landmark **Fish Roundabout** near Al Maktoum Hospital, which was the first purpose-built hospital on the Trucial Coast when it opened in 1949. It is hard to imagine that Burj Nahar was once a lone sentinel on the city's barren northern extremity, now that it is surrounded by lush greenery and residential buildings.

AROUND NAIF

The bustling heart of modern Deira is the Naif district, which lies between Omar Bin Al Khattab Road and the souks. While it is off the beaten track for most visitors, Naif has an interesting curiosity for history buffs: **Naif Museum** ⑬ (tel: 04 227 6484; Sat–Thur 8am–7.30pm, Fri 2.30–7.30pm;

Above from left:
defensive tower at
Deira's Naif Museum;
textile merchant at
Naif Souk; logo in the
pool at Dubai Creek
Golf & Yacht Club; the
iconic sails of the Golf
& Yacht Club.

charge) in **Naif Fort**, the first head-quarters of Dubai Police, when the force was established by Sheikh Rashid in 1956. You can reach it by walking for 20 minutes along Naif Road from Burj Nahar roundabout, but to save time and conserve energy you might want to catch another cab.

The fort, which remains a police station today, was added to a single square defensive tower constructed in 1939 to bolster the defence of the northern approach to Dubai. The original tower – made of coral stone, shells and gypsum – still stands, while the rest of the fort was reconstructed in 1994 on the orders of Sheikh Mohammed, who had been made head of Dubai Police and Public Security in 1968, when he was just 19.

The museum is housed in a room below the tower. Among the exhibits are early handguns and rifles, a stock restraint, known as Al Hataba, for prisoners' feet, and uniforms, including the current military-style green outfit and the first police *kandoura*, which was white with a red belt and red epaulettes.

Naif Souk
Directly behind Naif Fort is **Naif Souk** ⓮, where local men and women in national dress can be seen shopping for textiles sold by traders from Afghanistan and the Indian sub-continent. After exploring the museum and checking out the souk (you might want to return on a morning, when it is busier), hail another taxi and return to the Creek along Omar Bin Al Khattab Road.

THE GOLF & YACHT CLUB

There are two good spots in this area to enjoy a sundowner at the end of this tour. The first option is **The Aviation Club** ⓯, the leafy grounds of which are home to the **Irish Village**, see ⓣ④.

The **Aviation Club** hosts the two-week Association of Tennis Professionals (ATP) and World Tennis Association (WTA) Dubai Tennis Championships each February, when if you're lucky you might spot top-ranking players passing on their way to the tennis courts.

A second option is the popular canalside **Casper & Gambini's** restaurant, see ⓣ⑤, in Dubai Festival City, some 3 km (1.8 miles) further on.

Food and Drink 🍴

④ IRISH VILLAGE
The Aviation Club, Garhoud; tel: 04 282 4750;
ww.irishvillage.ae; daily 11am–2am; $$$
Opened in 1996, the 'IV' is a Dubai institution offering hearty pub grub and outdoor seating in a leafy setting complete with duck pond.

⑤ CASPAR & GAMBINI'S
Canal Walk, Ground Floor, Dubai Festival City; tel: 04 232 5850; open Sat–Thur 9am–midnight; Friday 10am–midnight; $$
Branch of the award-winning Lebanese chain of international restaurants, with indoor and outdoor dining right by the water's edge.

⑥ THE BOARDWALK
Dubai Creek Golf & Yacht Club, near Deira City Centre; tel: 04 295 6000; www.dubaigolf.com/creek; daily 8am–midnight; $$
As the name suggests, the outdoor seating extends over the Creek. The international menu is good, but it is the terrific marina with its Creek and city views that make this such a popular place at sundown.

Dubai Creek Golf & Yacht Club

Alternatively, you may prefer to end the day at **Dubai Creek Golf & Yacht Club** ⑯, an oasis in the middle of the city, the carefully manicured greens and fairways of which lie opposite Deira City Centre, one of Dubai's most popular malls. One of Dubai's two venues for the European Tour Dubai Desert Classic golf tournament, the club's course was originally created by American specialist Karl Litten (who also designed the Emirates Golf Club, *see p.18*); it was updated in 2004/5 by Thomas Björn and European Golf Design and is now a par-71 course. The lush lawns and adjoining marina give a real taste of Dubai's wealth.

To reach the club, take a taxi and ask the driver to drop you off at the golf clubhouse, easily recognisable by its a roof in the form of the sails of a traditional Arab dhow: a recurrent theme in Dubai architecture. The club's bar is open to the public and has a terrace that opens onto expansive verdant fairways with the Creek off to the right. You can either order drinks and stay here, or go back through the clubhouse and stroll past the Park Hyatt Dubai hotel towards the marina.

One of the best spots from which to watch the sunset is the golf club's **Boardwalk** restaurant, *see* ⑪⑥. Drink in hand, look west from the balcony to Creek Park and the silhouetted skyscrapers of Sheikh Zayed Road, or downriver to the office lights and neon signs of Deira.

Vintage Cars

On the way to Dubai International Airport, the ground floor of the Nasser Bin Abjullatif Al Serkal Building contains a display of historic vehicles (tel: 04 295 5000; Sat–Wed 8am–1pm and 4–7.30pm, Thur 8am–2pm; free) collected by the prominent Dubai trading family Al Serkal. Among the vehicles on display are Model T Fords, US military Willys Jeeps, Jeepneys from the Philippines and American classics such as the 1957 Buick Special and Chevrolet Fleetline.

Left: Dubai Creek Golf & Yacht Club.

NAD AL SHEBA
TO JUMEIRA

Nad Al Sheba Racecourse and Dubai's Camel Racetrack form the first part of a day-long driving itinerary that also takes in some of the world's tallest buildings, Jumeira Mosque, Sheikh Saeed's summer retreat and the splendid Burj Al Arab hotel.

Above: highlights of this tour: the iconic Burj Arab; a racing falcon; spectacular skyscrapers on Sheikh Zayed Road.

DISTANCE 33km (21 miles)
TIME A full day
START Nad Al Sheba Club
END Souk Madinat Jumeirah
POINTS TO NOTE

You will need a car *(see p.108)* for this itinerary. As the route demands an early start, it is best to arrange to pick up the car the evening before. From Jumeira/Deira/Bur Dubai, follow signs to Al Ain then Nad Al Sheba. The racecourse is on Muscat Street, to the right of the Dubai-Al Ain Road. Book in advance for the Nad Al Sheba Club Breakfast Stable Tour (tel: 04 336 3666), and remember to pack swimwear for the beach stop. Note the very early start to this tour.

Food and Drink 🍴
① SPIKES BAR
Nad Al Sheba Club; tel: 04 336 3666; www.nadalshebaclub.com; open from 7am; $$
Pleasant venue overlooking Nad Al Sheba Racecourse. The advantage is that you can have breakfast on the Spikes Bar terrace and watch the horses training.

This itinerary starts at Nad Al Sheba Racecourse, some 16km (10 miles) from downtown Bur Dubai. It is best to start early if you want to watch the early morning gallops.

NAD AL SHEBA RACECOURSE

Home to the world's richest horse race, the US$21.25 million Dubai World Cup, the **Nad Al Sheba Club ❶** (Nad Al Sheba; tel: 04 332 2277; free) showcases both the city's wealth and its legendary tradition of horse racing. Between 5 and 8am on most mornings from November to April you can watch thoroughbred and Arabian racehorses being put through their paces on their early-morning runs.

Even if you are not a fan of the sport of sheikhs, watching these magnificent beasts in such an impressive setting is an excellent way to start the day. (You can even track the horses whilst eating breakfast at **Spikes Bar**, *see* 🍴①.) The chances are you will be among only a handful of people, and the delicious blend of fresh air, birdsong, the whir of water sprinklers and drum of hooves works like caffeine on the soul.

Among the numerous stables and training tracks in the area, those that use the racecourse for training include the Nad Al Sheba, Green, Al Nasser, Moudesh and Maktoum stables. You might strike up a conversation with a trainer from one of them. Aside from the Dubai World Cup, which takes place annually in March, races are held on Thursday evenings between November and April. The lounge and terrace of the clubhouse next to the stand are open for breakfast from 7am, and its gift shop sells various Dubai World Cup hats, clothes and mementos.

Stable Tour

To get the most out of the morning session, join the **Nad Al Sheba Club's Breakfast Stable Tour**, which lasts from 7–11am, and costs Dhs170 per person (half price for children).

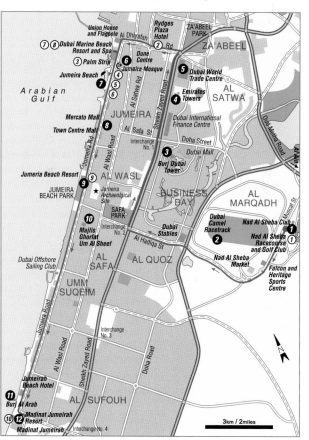

Robot Jockeys

Camel racing is a popular sport in Dubai but for many years it was the subject of an international debate about the use of young boys as camel jockeys. As a result, in 2004, the UAE Camel Racing Association ordered that riders under the age of 16 should be replaced with child-size, remote-controlled robot jockeys, developed by Swiss company K-Team. Apparently the camels cannot tell the difference.

Bedouin Camels
Historically, not only were camels used for getting around, but their milk and meat would provide valuable protein for an entire Bedu family for months on end. Camel hide was used to make bags and utensils, and the hair was woven into fine outer garments for men, known as *bisht*.

Below: sacks of camel feed at the Camel Racetrack.

CAMEL RACETRACK

Return to your car and set the odometer (mileometer) to zero, as for the next part of the tour, directions will be given in kilometres in addition to landmarks along the way. Head back through the car park to Muscat Street. At 1.9km (1.1 miles) you will pass the **Falcon and Heritage Sports Centre** (daily 10am–11pm), where hunting falcons are sold to registered falconers. Visitors are welcome to view and even hold the birds. At 2.1km (1.3 miles) turn right towards **Nad Al Sheba Market**, home to fodder traders, veterinary clinics and general stores; park the car here.

The next main stop, the **Camel Racetrack ❷** (Nad Al Sheba Racecourse; tel: 04 338 8170; races held Thur 7.30am and 2pm and Fri 7.30am and 2.30pm; free), is on your right. At this time of day (mid-morning) you are likely to see processions of racing camels, reminiscent of Bedouin camel trains, ambling back to the stables after training.

At the Racetrack

Camel racing is immensely popular in Dubai, and its revival in recent years, supported by Sheikh Mohammed, has preserved an ancient tradition that was almost wiped out by the oil boom. A visit to the packed racetrack offers a fascinating glimpse into local life. Be sure to arrive promptly, as the races are quite short – a 10-km (6-mile) race is over in fewer than 20 minutes. Although betting on races is strictly forbidden, cash prizes are awarded to winners, and a fast camel can change hands for millions of *dirhams*.

Before returning to your car, take some time to explore the small shops in the market. Here you can barter for exceptionally good-value camel blankets and other items associated with the sport, from whips and muzzles to intricately patterned camel saddles.

TOWARDS JUMEIRA

Zero the odometer for the next leg at the junction and head for the coast at **Jumeira**, a 15-km (9-mile) drive away. Early in the day, it should take no longer than 30 minutes, but there are a few sights on the way.

Turn right at the junction and you will see that the road forks almost immediately. Take the left fork (the right leads to the grandstand) and continue on this road until you reach Interchange No. 2 on the Dubai-Abu Dhabi Road at 4.7km (2.9 miles). Along the way, you will see **Dubai Stables**, to the right at 4.3km (2.6 miles). Note that the speed limit here is 60kph (37mph).

SHEIKH ZAYED ROAD

At the interchange, take the right slip road at 4.7km (2.9 miles) and feed onto the highway heading towards Dubai and Sharjah. The speed limit here is 100kph (62mph).

Burj Dubai

At around 7.3km (4.5 miles), **Burj Dubai** ❸ *(see right)*, is visible to your right. Designed by Adrian Smith of the Chicago firm Skidmore, Owings and Merrill, it will be the tallest building in the world when completed. The exact height has been a closely guarded secret during construction, but it is expected to top 700m (2,296ft).

Emirates Towers and Dubai World Trade Centre

At 8.5km (5.2 miles) you pass under Interchange No. 1 and enter the corridor of tall buildings along Sheikh Zayed Road, visible from the racetrack. At 10.2km (6.3 miles) you will see to the

Above from left:
Camel Racetrack; real-estate development in Jumeira.

Burj Dubai
This spiralling skyscraper will be the tallest building in the world on completion. The building, the base of which is inspired by the geometry of a desert flower, is visible from up to 95km (59 miles) away. It will house the world's first Armani Hotel (www. armanihotels.com) and the highest observation deck in the world.

21st-Century Falcons

The fastest creatures on the planet have been trained for hunting in Arabia for thousands of years, but in the 21st century the ancient skill of falconry is maintained for sport rather than survival. Before weapons, saker falcons and peregrine falcons – which can achieve speeds of 320kph (199mph) in a dive – were used by Bedu hunters to catch food. Wild falcons migrating through the Gulf States were caught and trained in two or three weeks at the start of the hunting season in October. Favoured prey was the houbara bustard, a desert bird the size of a heron whose meat could be vital to a family's survival. At the end of the season, in March, the falcon would be freed. Today, falcons are increasingly no longer captured, but bred in captivity. Even so, they require human contact on a daily basis, or else they become wild and unreliable. Especially keen falconers fly to Pakistan for hunting expeditions, their falcons travelling on their own special passports. Falcons are also put to practical use: Dubai's Burj Al Arab hotel employs a falconer to keep pigeons – and pigeon droppings – off the landmark property.

right the twin silver-grey metal-and-glass **Emirates Towers** ❹, the larger of which was once, at 350m (1,148ft), the tallest building in the Middle East and Europe, and the white **Dubai World Trade Centre** ❺, the city's first major building project, which was completed in the 1970s.

Towards Jumeira

You now need to follow the signs for Za'abeel and Bur Dubai, so keep right. At 11.1km (6.8 miles) take a right slip road off the highway and bear left around the roundabout to the fifth exit, following signs to Jumeira. You are now on Al Dhiyafah Road. Take the middle lane for Jumeira.

At Al Satwa Roundabout at 13.3km (8.2 miles), you will see the **Rydges Plaza Hotel** to your right. The hotel's restaurants and bars include the ever-popular Tex-Mex **Cactus Cantina**, *see* ⑪②, which offers a good view over the districts of Satwa and Jumeira.

The Dune Centre

Go straight across at the roundabout, continuing along Al Dhiyafah Road. You are now in that rare thing in a city of malls – a shopping street. At 13.8km (8.5 miles), to your left, is the **Dune Centre**, a shopping mall.

Fountain Roundabout

At the traffic lights and **Fountain Roundabout**, ignore the first sign for Jumeira and Umm Suqeim, which leads up Al Wasl Road, but follow the second, up Jumeira Road. At the junction, the flagpole and Union House mark the spot where UAE independence was declared in 1971, while ahead to the left are the minarets of the **Jumeira Mosque** ❻, whose image appears on UAE's Dhs500 bank note. Built of stone in the medieval Fatimid style in the 1970s, it is the city's largest mosque and the only one that non-Muslims may enter, through the **Sheikh Mohammed Centre for Cultural Understanding** (tel: 04 353 6666; tours Sat, Sun, Tue and Thur 10am; *see walk 10, p.70*). At 15.3km (9.5 miles), turn right towards Dubai Marine Beach Resort & Spa (*see p.110*), and park the car.

JUMEIRA

Jumeira and the neighbouring district of **Umm Suqeim**, which tends to be thought of as part of Jumeira, is similar to Los Angeles' Venice Beach and Orange County rolled into one. One of the city's wealthiest residential areas, it is home to many of the rich expats who live in Dubai. A sizeable Muslim community also lives in Jumeira, hence the density of mosques here.

A number of attractions – west-facing beaches (gathering places at sunset), restaurants, cafés, small shopping malls, sailing clubs, a waterfront park, water theme park and hotels, some of which are superlative – draw visitors to create

Food and Drink

② CACTUS CANTINA

Rydges Plaza Hotel, Al Dhiyafah Street, Satwa Roundabout; tel: 04 398 2274; daily noon–1am; $$
Tex Mex/Nuevo Latino food. Salsa dancing on Sat/Sun from 8pm; Thur cheap drinks for women.

an appealing seaside atmosphere that is removed from the bustle of the city.

Jumeira Beach

The European wives of the Jumeira/ Umm Suqeim set are known locally as 'Jumeira Janes', though this rather disparaging nickname is now almost as questionable as 'Moscow Beach', the name once given to **Jumeira Beach ❼** because of the large number of Russians who used to gather here.

The next few hours of the tour can be spent in the vicinity of this public

Above from far left: Sheikh Zayed Road skyline, from Trade Centre Roundabout to Interchange No.1; Armani making a mark in Dubai.

The Palm and The World

Dubai's citizens like to think big when it comes to building projects. Until recently, the most famous of these was the sail-shaped Burj Al-Arab (Tower of the Arabs), the only seven-star hotel in the world, with a lobby tall enough to accommodate the Eiffel Tower. Now, 6km (4 miles) off the Emirates coast, three artificial palm-shaped islands have been built that are so large that they can be seen from space with the naked eye. Palm Jumeirah and Palm Jebel Ali, give Dubai an additional 120km (75 miles) of sandy beach and house super-deluxe hotels, around 4,000 exclusive villas (each with its own private stretch of beach), plus water parks, marinas, shopping malls, health spas and entertainment complexes. Palm Jebel Jumeirah has 17 fronds, a 2-km (1¼-mile) trunk and an arc-like breakwater measuring 11km (7 miles) from end to end, which offers a sheltered habitat for tropical fish. Palm Jebel Ali, which is larger than Palm Jumeirah, has a ring of water homes on stilts, arranged in such a fashion as to spell out a verse from a poem *(Take wisdom from the wise people – not everyone who rides is a jockey)* by Sheikh Mohammed, the original driving force behind the Palm developments. The third palm-shaped island, The Palm Deira, which is underway, will be the largest of the palm-tree developments, measuring 14km (8½ miles) in length and 8.5 km (5 miles) wide, with 41 fronds on which will eventually stand some 8,000 two-storey villas, plus high-profile offices, leisure amenities, etc.

Nakheel, the property developer in charge of the Palms, has pushed the land reclamation even concept further with its latest grand project: 'The World', a mini-archipelago of 250–300 islands, some for private-ownership, others housing small, exclusive communities, arranged in the shape of a world map.

Above from left:
Majlis Ghorfat Um Al
Sheef; Mercato Mall.

World Records
Dubai is associated
with some 35
Guinness world
records, including the
largest gathering of
people with the same
name, set by 1,500
Mohammeds in 2005.

beach, just adjacent to the Dubai Marine Beach Resort & Spa. (Note that on certain days the beach is reserved for women only.)

If you are hungry at this point, there are several good options. For a light bite, the **Japengo Café**, *see* ⑪③, in the Palm Strip shopping mall on Jumeira Road offers fine views towards the Jumeira Mosque. Alternatively, sample the delights of **Gerard**, *see* ⑪④. In a

distinctive lime-colour converted villa on this side of the Spinneys super-market is the **Lime Tree Café**, *see* ⑪⑤, an expat favourite. Or you might try Café **Le Nôtre Paris**, *see* ⑪⑥, located within the Spinneys building.

For something a little more substan-tial, choose Dubai Marine Beach Resort & Spa's Tex-Mex **El Paso** restaurant, *see* ⑪⑦, or the resort's **Taverna** Mediter-ranean restaurant, *see* ⑪⑧.

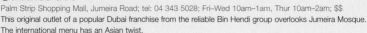

Food and Drink

③ JAPENGO CAFÉ
Palm Strip Shopping Mall, Jumeira Road; tel: 04 343 5028; Fri–Wed 10am–1am, Thur 10am–2am; $$
This original outlet of a popular Dubai franchise from the reliable Bin Hendi group overlooks Jumeira Mosque. The international menu has an Asian twist.

④ GERARD
Magrudy's Mall, Jumeira Beach Road; tel: 04 344 3327; daily 7.30am–1am; $
This European-style coffee shop is a perennially popular meeting place for people of all nationalities.

⑤ LIME TREE CAFÉ
Near Spinneys, Jumeira Road; tel: 04 349 8498; daily 7.30am–6pm; $–$$
Reminiscent of an arts centre café, the understatedly hip Lime Tree occupies two floors of a stylish villa with out-door seating. Healthy specialities include outstanding carrot cake in Dubai, tasty wraps and delicious smoothies.

⑥ LE NÔTRE PARIS
Spinney Centre, Jumeira Road; tel: 04 349 4433; daily 8am–midnight; $$$
Chic and elegant French restaurant with an intimate atmosphere. Cheaper cafe downstairs with a larger upscale restaurant above.

⑦ EL PASO
Marine Beach & Spa, 5182 Jumeira Beach Road; tel: 04 304 8120; noon– 11.30pm; $–$$
Lively Tex-Mex restaurant restaurant and bar with DJ and live entertainment every night, such as tribute singers/comedians and a quiz night. The restaurant serves both à la carte and buffet food.

⑧ TAVERNA
Marine Beach & Spa, 5182 Jumeira Beach Road; tel: 04 304 8130; open 24 hours; $$–$$$
Dine on the shaded terrace and enjoy a wide-ranging international menu, from Indonesian to French to traditional English fish and chips.

⑨ SHU
Jumeira Road, opposite Jumeirah Beach Park; tel: 04 349 1303; Sun–Thur 10am–3 or 4am; $$
A trendy Lebanese café named after the Arabic for 'What?' Inside there's a nightclub vibe, but outside on the terrace it's relaxed. If you're feeling adventurous, try the house speciality: fried sparrow with pomegranate syrup.

Alternatively, assuming it is not during the 30 days of Ramadan, when you should not eat in public in daylight hours, you may like to take a picnic to the beach. You will find all the ingredients you require at the Spinneys supermarket across the road.

Afternoon Walk

After lunch, a walk along the breakwater at the end of the beach offers a fine view back to the city's skyline, the commercial towers of Sheikh Zayed Road contrasting with the frivolity of beach life in the foreground. Further up the coast lies today's final destination: **Souk Madinat Jumeirah**. Next to it, and just visible from here, is **Burj Al Arab** *(see p.50)*, one of the world's tallest hotels, built on its own island.

TWO OPTIONS

At this point you may like either to stay on the beach for another hour or so or catch up with the itinerary later at Sheikh Saeed's former summer retreat Majlis Ghorfat Um Al Sheef. The following directions apply to both options.

Back at the car park alongside Dubai Marine Beach Resort & Spa, zero the odometer, then follow the one-way system parallel to the beach. At 0.6km (0.3 miles), turn left towards Jumeira Road. Bear in mind that the speed limit on Jumeira Road is 80kph (50mph).

1) Mercato Mall and Jumeira Beach Park

At 2.1km (1.3 miles) from Dubai Marine Beach Resort & Spa is the Italian-inspired **Mercato Mall 8**. At 2.5km (1.5 miles), on a side-street just after Town Centre Mall, you will see the Creative Art Centre, where Arabic antiques, curios and art can be bought. At 4.1km (2.5 miles) you will pass the exclusive **Jumeira Beach Resort 9**, which played host to the England football squad en route to the 2002 Japan World Cup. At 4.8km (2.9 miles) is the entrance to **Jumeira Beach Park**, which has a very pleasant public beach. For a bite to eat here, try **Shu**, *see* ⑪⑨.

2) Majlis Ghorfat Um Al Sheef

At 7km (4.3 miles) do a U-turn, then, at 7.9km (4.9 miles), turn right onto 17 Street. Our next stop, **Majlis Ghorfat Um Al Sheef 10** (tel: 04 394 6343; Sat–Thur 8.30am–8.30pm, Fri 2.30–8.30pm; charge), also known as Majlis Al Ghoraifa, is a short way along on the left.

Above: Jumeira statue, café and supermarket.

Below: Majlis Ghorfat Um Al Sheef.

Above from left: pier to the idyllic Pierchic restaurant *(see p.120–1)* at the Al Qasr Hotel; Madinat Jumeirah Resort.

Below: Andre Agassi and Roger Federer playing tennis on the helipad of Burj Al Arab.

Originally constructed in 1955 when the surrounding area was nothing more than date palm groves and fishing shacks, the *majlis* ('meeting place') served as the summer resort of the former ruler Sheikh Saeed and his son Sheikh Rashid. It is possible that this traditional, two-storey structure – with its verandas, teak doors and windows, and simple comforts – was where modern Dubai was conceived. The *majlis* served as a police station in the 1960s but has since been restored to its former glory with the addition of a *falaj* irrigation system in the gardens.

BURJ AL ARAB

Zero the odometer for the last leg of the journey to **Souk Madinat Jumeirah**. Turning right from 17 Street into the flow of traffic, do a U-turn at 0.3km (0.18 mile) and head for the setting sun.

At the traffic lights at 6.2km (3.8 miles) take a right on Al Thanya Street for a brief detour to admire the billowing sail-shaped building that is the super-luxurious (seven-star) **Burj Al Arab ⓫** ('Arabian Tower') hotel from another of the city's public beaches.

Impressive Statistics

Located some 280m/yds offshore, on its own man-made island and reached via a private causeway, the Burj Al Arab is, at 321m (1,053ft), taller than Paris's Eiffel Tower and a mere 60m (200ft) shorter than the Empire State Building in New York. Opened in 1999 and already an icon, this incredible feat of engineering has 28 double-height storeys (all 202 suites are duplexes and each has its own butler) and the world's tallest atrium behind a sail façade, which complements the 'wave' design of the nearby Jumeirah Beach Hotel.

Constructed with double-Teflon-coated glass fibre, the sail is dazzling white by day but in the evening becomes an extraordinary canvas for spectacular light displays.

The space-age helicopter pad jutting out from the top floor was famously used as a practice driving range by Tiger

Woods and as a tennis court by Roger Federer and Andre Agassi. Other celebrities to have stayed in the Dhs6,500-a-night suites include Hollywood stars Brad Pitt and Angelina Jolie.

Burj Al Arab restricts access to hotel guests or those who have booked a table at one of its restaurants. These include the fabulous Al Muntaha (literally 'The Highest'), 200m (656ft) above the Arabian Gulf with breathtaking views of the coast.

MADINAT JUMEIRAH

Returning to Jumeira Road via Al Thanya/325 Street, turn right. After passing the wave-shaped **Jumeirah Beach Hotel** *(see p.110)*, once voted the world's best by readers of *Condé Nast Traveller* magazine, and Wild Wadi Water Park *(see p.21)*, at 1.5km (0.9 miles) from the beach turn right into the fabulous Arabian-themed **Madinat Jumeirah Resort** ⑫ (literally Jumeirah City Resort).

The Resort

Opened in 2004, the resort has two luxury hotels – Mina A'Salam (literally 'Port of Peace') and Al Qasr ('The Castle'), both of which have jaw-droppingly beautiful interior décor and a number of licensed restaurants and bars, including **Al Makan**, *see* ⑪⑩, which are in idyllic sea-view settings and open to non-guests.

The resort also has a lovely covered market, **Souk Madinat Jumeirah** (daily 10am–11pm), which despite its recent construction manages to convey an authentic atmosphere. As well as various antiques shops, clothing boutiques and handicraft stalls, the souk has a number of bars, licensed restaurants and cafés that spread onto picturesque terraces, and one of Dubai's best nightclubs, Trilogy.

There is also a small art gallery, Gallery One, which showcases paintings, mixed-media art and photography by local and international artists; past exhibitors include the iconic 1960s photographer Terry O'Neill. A network of canals, serviced by *abra* water taxis for guest-use only, links the hotels and Al Qasr's 29 wind-tower summer houses with the souk and various waterfront restaurants.

Madinat Jumeirah also has a grand theatre and a large exhibition hall, which has hosted the likes of Bjorn Borg and John McEnroe in exhibition tennis tournaments. The resort provides an opulent setting for the Dubai International Film Festival in December, which serves as a cultural bridge between film-makers and stars from Hollywood, Bollywood and the Middle East film industry.

Madinat Jumeirah
Thai architect Thanu Boonyawatana likened his approach to that of a movie special-effects wizard, who, with the aid of computer-generated imagery, recreates ancient Greece or Rome for cinema audiences. 'We thought, 'What if in ancient UAE or ancient Oman they had the money we have now and the technology we have now? What would they have built?' We built what they might have built…'

Food and Drink

⑩ AL MAKAN
Souk Madinat Jumeirah; tel: 04 368 6593; www.alkoufa.com; daily noon–1am; $$
Located in an atmospheric souk, Al Makan is one of the few restaurants in Dubai serving authentic Emirati cuisine. Lebanese mezze also available. Outdoor terrace seating overlooks Burj Al Arab hotel.

HERITAGE SIGHTS

This itinerary travels back in time, heading straight for the historic heart of Dubai with visits to attractions on both sides of Dubai Creek in Shindagha, Bur Dubai and Deira, as well as the ruins of a pre-Islamic trading post in Jumeira.

Above: Dubai Museum; old and new in Bastakiya, visited at the end of this tour.

Below: taking a walk along the Shindagha waterfront.

DISTANCE 14km (9 miles)
TIME A full day
START Sheik Saaed Al Maktoum House
END Jumeira Archaeological Site
POINTS TO NOTE

This tour has a mixture of directions to walk, take public transport and taxis between sights (definitely a better option for the longest leg rather than trying to park a rental car in Dubai's narrow streets). The fare will be around Dhs30. We will also be crossing the Creek on an *abra* (water taxi); fare: Dh1 per person. Note that this tour is best done from Saturday to Thursday, as that is when the Sheikh Saeed Al Maktoum House, a highlight of the itinerary, is open all day.

This is the heritage tour to choose if time is tight or you prefer concentrated bouts of sightseeing. (For speedy sightseeing, this walk is a great alternative to tours 1 and 2, which give more protracted coverage of the same historic area.) It is a good option for those who want to see all Dubai's historic sights in one go, leaving the rest of the time in the city free for the beach and shops. It is also one for dedicated history buffs.

SHINDAGHA

Our starting point is the area of **Shindagha**, the curling promontory at the mouth of the creek that is the most likely site of the original fishing and pearling village, which would have consisted of simple palm-frond dwellings called *barasti* or *arish*, and perhaps a few mud-brick houses.

The main residential area for Dubai's Arab population in the 1800s and early 1900s, Shindagha was the traditional seat of the community's leaders. It was here in 1823 that Mohammed Bin Hazza welcomed the Persia-based British Political Resident in the Gulf, Lieutenant J. McLeod, and learnt of British intentions to place a representative agent in the more established settlement of Sharjah, to the north.

The Al Maktoums

It was here, too, that 800 members of the Al Bu Falasah sub-section of the Bani Yas tribe settled after seceding from Abu Dhabi in 1833. Led by Sheikh Maktoum Bin Buti and Sheikh Obaid Bin Saeed Bin Rashid, the Bani Yas influx transformed the politics of a community that had numbered around 1,200 people before their arrival. Maktoum became its new ruler, establishing at Shindagha the Al Maktoum dynasty that rules Dubai to this day.

SHEIKH SAEED'S HOUSE

The Maktoum family's former home (built in 1896 for Sheikh Maktoum Bin Hasher Al Maktoum but now named after his successor Sheikh Saeed, who ruled the emirate from 1912 to 1958) was rebuilt between 1984 and 1986 and, under the name **Sheikh Saeed Al Maktoum House ❶** (tel: 04 393 7139; Sat–Thur 8am– 8.30pm; Fri 3–9.30pm; charge), is a museum of early life in Dubai. It contains photographs, an exhibition on fishing and pearling, coins, stamps and historic documents.

Architectural Highlights

The two-storey structure, built from coral stone and covered in lime and sand-coloured plaster, is an impressive example of late 19th-century Arabian architecture, with Persian and Islamic influences. Architectural features include vaulted, high-beamed ceilings, arched doorways, sculpted window overhangs and carved trellis screens, but the overriding feature of the house is its four *barjeel*, or wind-towers, an innovative, early form of

Coffee-Drinking

Gulf coffee *(kahwa)* is made from green coffee beans, is very strong and may be flavoured with cardamom or saffron. Poured from a distinctive pot, it is served in tiny cups without handles, which are refilled until the drinker 'wobbles' the cup from side to side, indicating that they have had sufficient. Three cups is the polite number to drink, indicating pleasure in the coffee but not excess.

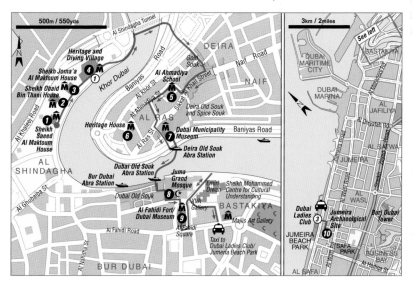

Above from left: detail of a fine arch on Al Ahmadiya School, Dubai's first and now a museum of education; slippers in front of a clothing store in Deira.

air conditioning introduced to Dubai by traders from Persia.

RENOVATED HOUSES

The beautification of this stretch of the Creek that followed the rebuilding of Sheikh Saeed's house has included the reconstruction of two other heritage houses. The first, **Sheikh Obaid Bin Thani House ❷** (tel: 04 223 0000; hours vary; free), dates from 1916, and preserves both architectural heritage and cultural and religious traditions. Exhibitions and programmes are run here with the aim of promoting a greater understanding of Islam.

The second, the adjacent **Sheikh Joma'a Al Maktoum House ❸** (tel: 04 393 7151; Sun–Thur 8am–8.30pm; Fri 3–8.30pm; charge), dates from 1928 and contains historical images of the emirate and a collection of stamps, coins and other currency used for trade in the early 20th century.

HERITAGE AND DIVING VILLAGE

The area is also home to the **Heritage and Diving Village ❹** (tel: 04 393 7151; Sat–Thur 8am–10pm; Fri 8–11am, 4–10pm; free), a short walk north of Sheikh Saeed's House *(see p.53)*, where various aspects of architecture, agriculture and the traditions of the UAE are recreated, from the mountain houses of the Hatta region to performances by local bands daily at 4.30pm between October and April. Note that a good pitstop at this point is **Al Bandar**, see ⑪①.

Below: details of old dwellings in the Heritage Village.

TOWARDS DEIRA

From here, continue along the promenade, towards the mouth of the Creek, and take the pedestrian tunnel under the waterway to **Deira**. Early dwellings in Deira were made of palm fronds, but after fire ravaged the community in 1894 more substantial homes were constructed, using coral stone and gypsum. By 1908, according to the historian and geographer G.G. Lorimer, there were 1,600 houses and 350 shops in Deira, compared to just 200 houses and 50 shops in Bur Dubai.

A Developing District

Together with Bur Dubai, Deira formed the commercial heart of old Dubai, but it was also the district where new services emerged: the children of Shindagha and Bur Dubai crossed to Deira for an education, after the city's first school was established here in 1912, and people came to Deira for medical treatment after the first hospital on the Trucial Coast, Al Maktoum Hospital, was established here in 1949.

AL AHMADIYA SCHOOL

Resisting the lure of Deira's famous Gold Souk (for more of this, *see tour 2, p.36*), head for **Al Ahmadiya School** ❺ (tel: 04 226 0286; Sat–Thur 8am–7.30pm; Fri 2.30–7.30pm; free), located on Al Ahmadiya Street in the Al Ras area, a short walk from the souk. (From the tunnel exit, head straight through the car park towards the wooden roof of the Gold Souk. Inside the souk, turn right onto Sikkat Al Khail Street. As you exit the souk, turn right again onto Old Baladiya Street. Follow the street as it curves to the left.)

First School in Dubai

When it was established in 1912, Al Ahmadiya School was the first semi-formal school in Dubai, and, when formal education was introduced in 1956, it was one of the emirate's first regular schools. Prior to the school's establishment by local pearl merchant Ahmad Bin Dalmouk, after whom it was named, boys were taught the Koran, Arabic calligraphy and arithmetic in their own homes by a man or woman known as *al muttawa* – literally 'volunteer'.

With the establishment along the Trucial Coast of semi-formal schools, typically financed by pearl merchants *(al tawaweesh)*, the curriculum was expanded to include such subjects as mathematics, sciences, history, literature and astronomy.

Above: cargo on the Deira Creekside; example of a traditional dwelling.

Food and Drink 🍴
① AL BANDAR
Heritage Village, Shindagha; tel: 04 393 9001; daily 11am–1am; $$
This unlicensed restaurant in the Heritage Area is an ideal place to sit outside and watch the *abras* ply the waters of the Creek on a balmy evening. The emphasis is on international seafood dishes, but there are also meat and vegetarian choices; large buffet served at weekends.

Famous Alumni
Among the school's illustrious alumni are Sheikh Rashid Bin Saeed Al Maktoum, 'the Father of Dubai', who worked relentlessly to modernize the city as ruler between 1958 and 1990, and Sheikh Mohammed Bin Rashid Al Maktoum, UAE vice president, prime minister and ruler of Dubai, who has masterminded the city's impressive development.

Above from left:
Municipality Museum;
the view over the
rooftops from Al Fahidi
Fort; entrance to the
Historical Buildings
Section of the
Municipality Museum.

Evolution

Built in three phases, Al Ahmadiya School was initially a single-storey structure with 11 classrooms and a *liwan*, or veranda, around an inner courtyard. The upper floor was added in 1920. In 1932, following the collapse of the pearl trade, and with it the local economy, the school was forced to close, but it reopened in 1937 with a government subsidy.

In 1956, with the introduction of a formal education system for boys (1958 for girls), schools were expected to follow a regular curriculum that included English, sociology and more science subjects. Student numbers increased, and, by 1962, the school had 823 students – more than it could comfortably accommodate. In 1963, when it moved to a new, larger site, the original building was closed.

Recent Restoration

During its restoration by Dubai Municipality's Historical Buildings Section from 1995, authentic building materials such as coral stone, gypsum and sandalwood were used to recreate Al Ahmadiya School, as its famous old boys would have known it. The school has been used to house a museum of education since 2000.

HERITAGE HOUSE

Next to Al Ahmadiya School is **Heritage House ⑥** (tel: 04 226 0216; Sat–Thur 8am–7.30pm; Fri 2.30–7.30pm; free), which was also restored in the mid-1990s and opened to the public in 2000. The former residence of the Bin Dalmouk family, the pearl traders who established the school, the oldest part of Heritage House dates back to 1890, when it was built for Mohammed Bin Saeed Bin Muzaaina. Sheikh Ahmad Bin Dalmouk expanded the house when he assumed ownership in 1910.

Traditional Emirati Home

Today, the 935-sq-m (10,065-sq-ft) building is preserved as it would have been in the 1940s and 1950s. It is one of best surviving examples of a traditional Emirati home and provides a snapshot of the social life of Dubai's wealthier inhabitants during that period. Notable features include the separate men's and women's *majlis*, or meeting rooms, where guests would sit on embroidered silk or wool pillows around the edge of a Persian-carpeted floor, drinking Arabic coffee and discussing the economic, social and political issues of the day.

MUNICIPALITY MUSEUM

The modern home of Dubai Municipality is on the Creekside next to the Radisson SAS Hotel, but its former headquarters has been preserved as another of Deira's heritage buildings. Located on the edge of the Spice Souk, across Baniyas Road from the Deira Old Souk Abra Station, the **Municipality Museum ⑦** (tel: 04 225 3312; Sat–Thur 8.30am–8.30pm; Fri 4–8.30pm; free) is a simple but elegant, two-storey structure with a long wooden balcony that recalls the period buildings of New Orleans' French

Quarter. Restored in 1999, this former local government headquarters is now a museum of municipality history (see p.37).

square, high- walled compound with corner towers covered in sun-baked plaster – is an arresting, if apparently care-worn, sight among the modern

JUMA GRAND MOSQUE

From here, we cross the road to catch an *abra* (water taxi) from Deira Old Souk Abra Station back across the Creek to the Bur Dubai Abra Station, and walk through the old textile souk towards the landmark **Juma Grand Mosque** ❽ (Muslims only). The mosque is not only one of the oldest in Dubai (it dates to 1900, although it was rebuilt in 1998), it also has the city's tallest minaret (70m/231ft), nine large domes, 45 small domes and space for 1,200 worshippers.

AL FAHIDI FORT

In the square in front of the Grand Mosque is the oldest surviving structure in Bur Dubai, **Al Fahidi Fort** ❾, which was built between 1787 and 1799 to guard the landward approach to the town. The Portuguese-influenced fortress served as the ruler's residence and the seat of government in the past, and would have been a refuge for the inhabitants of the coastal community in the event of attack. At one time, it was also the city jail.

Dubai Museum

Since 1971, the fort has housed **Dubai Museum** (tel: 04 353 1862; Sat–Thur 8.30am–8.30pm, Fri 2.30–8.30pm; charge). The building itself – a simple,

Pearl Diving

Before 'black gold' there were pearls. In the centuries before oil was discovered, pearling was the mainstay of the Dubai economy, involving the majority of the creek settlements' male population. From June to September boats of between 15 and 60 men stayed at sea for up to four months, moving from one pearl oyster bed to another and sheltering from storms on Gulf islets. Equipped with little more than a nose clip, ear plugs and finger pads, and surviving on a diet of fish and rationed water, the men would dive on weighted ropes to depths of around 15m (49ft) up to 50 times a day. In two or three minutes under water they could collect up to a dozen pearl oysters. Pearls were graded according to their size, colour and shape. In the early 20th century, the best pearls or *jiwan* (a derivative of 'Grade One' or 'G-One') could fetch 1,500 rupees, but while Dubai's pearl merchants grew wealthy, a diver's wages for the entire season could be as little as 30–60 rupees. Famous for their rose-colouring, Dubai pearls were traded in India, from where they were sent to Paris. The popularity of the Japanese cultured pearl from the 1930s devastated the Gulf industry. It struggled on for another decade, but the last great pearling expedition sailed from Dubai in 1949.

apartment blocks and office buildings of Al Fahidi Street. On the plaza beside it stands a stunning replica of the wooden pearling dhows that were used in the 18th and 19th centuries.

The surprise within the museum is the quality of the exhibits, most of which are displayed in underground galleries added to the museum in 1995. From the multi-media overview of the development of Dubai to the detailed dioramas recreating scenes from everyday life in the years before oil, the creative, contemporary presentation of its exhibits makes this museum an unexpected gem. Among the artefacts shown here are finds from the archaeological sites at Al Qusais and Jumeira, dating from the Iron Age and 6th century.

BASTAKIYA

No visit to Dubai would be complete without a visit to 'historic' Bastakiya. Until the mid-1990s this was a run-down neighbourhood with scores of poorly paid Asian expatriates crammed into dilapidated wind-tower houses. However, thanks to a restoration programme undertaken by Dubai Municipality's Historical Buildings Section from 1996, Bastakiya has become a case study for urban conservation in the Arab world.

Early Traders

Located on the Creekside next to the Emiri Diwan, or Ruler's Palace, Bastakiya would not have been built were it not for the city's open-door policy to foreign trade. Its original residents were wealthy traders from Bastak and Lingah on the coast of modern-day Iran – hence the name. They settled here, close to their shops in the nearby souk, between 1902 and 1950, the period in which the 25 surviving wind-tower houses were built.

Wind-Towers

The wind-towers, which can rise to a height of 15m (49ft), were an early

Below: women head out shopping in Bastakiya.

form of air conditioning: the four open sides of each square tower caught the breeze and channelled it into rooms below. The walls of each house were made of coral stone, which, thanks to its porous nature, has low thermal conductivity, keeping temperatures inside to a minimum.

For privacy and security, there were no windows on the ground floor, just a few ventilation holes, which gives the narrow *sikka* (alleyways) between the brown, plaster-covered buildings an Arabian Nights ambience. It is possible to enter several of these courtyard houses, which now contain art galleries, small museums and restaurants.

PRE-ISLAMIC RUINS

Outside the Majlis Art Gallery, one of the early Bastakiya homes on Al Fahidi Road *(see p.29)*, hail a taxi and ask for **Dubai Ladies Club/Jumeira Beach Park**. Inland from the ladies club and park, in a residential neighbourhood between Jumeira Road and Al Wasl Road, is our final destination, **Jumeira Archaeological Site ❿**.

To get here from the ladies club entrance, cross Jumeira Road at the traffic lights and walk up 27 Street, which is almost opposite the ladies club entrance, then turn right on 16 Street. You will see the entrance to the site 200m/yds ahead on the left. (If it is too hot to walk for 15 minutes, navigate your way in a taxi by taking the next U-turn after the Ladies Club and following the same directions up 27 Street.)

Jumeira Archaeological Site

One of the Arabian Gulf's most significant archaeological sites, these ruins of a trading post date back more than 1,000 years, but were first uncovered by archaeologists in 1969. The original settlement, strategically positioned on the ancient trade route between Mesopotamia and Oman, dates back to the pre-Islamic Sassanid era, which ended in the 7th century AD. The site was built on and expanded by the Abbasids in the first two or three centuries of the Islamic era and is today one of the largest and most important early Islamic sites in the Gulf.

Among the excavated ruins are the foundations of several houses, including the Sassanid-era governor's palace, market buildings, a large *caravanserai* in which travellers would meet and carry out business, and also a small mosque.

JUMEIRA ROAD

After viewing the ruins, head back to Jumeira Road to catch a taxi back to your hotel, or shake off the past with a refreshing drink at the **Shu** café *(see ⑪⑨, p.48)*, opposite the beach park, or at **Malecon**, see ⑪③.

Above from far left: Bastakiya is known for its historic windtowers; Emirati man walking through backstreets; Jumeira Archaeological Site.

Food and Drink

③ MALECON

Dubai Marine Beach Resort & Spa, Jumeira Beach Road; tel: 04 346 1111; daily 7pm–3am; $$$

After a dose of heritage and culture, let your hair down at one of Dubai's hippest hot spots serving Cuban-Fusion food. The place livens up later in the night with the live salsa band (and an instructor on hand for those wishing to learn a few steps).

5 A HELICOPTER TOUR

The most exciting way to see Dubai in one swoop is by helicopter. Specific routes vary, depending on timing and conditions, hence the tour cannot be plotted exactly on a map, but the main points in terms of the practicalities and what you can expect to see are covered here.

TIME 30 minutes for the tour; allow 1½ hours in total
START/END Terminal 2, Dubai International Airport
POINTS TO NOTE
Take a taxi to the VIP Terminal, near the Airport Expo at Dubai International Airport (not to be confused with the main arrivals and departures terminal, which is in a separate location). Thereafter, your mode of transport will be a Bell 206 helicopter flying at an altitude of 457m (1,500ft). Book at least three days in advance with Aerogulf Services; tel: 04 220 0331; fax: 04 220 0924. You will need your passport both for booking and on the day of your flight.

The experience of sitting in a Bell 206 helicopter and seeing Dubai's landmarks pass by through the Perspex under your feet is like taking a ride over the city centre and along the coast in a great glass elevator. The perfect punctuation mark after the various one-day itineraries, this tour encompasses virtually everything you will have seen and puts the routes you have covered into perspective. On top of all that, it is really the only way to see the Palm Jumeirah *(see p.47 and photograph opposite)* in all its glory and appreciate what a mammoth undertaking this palm-tree shaped land reclamation project was.

Practicalities

Aerogulf Services, a Dubai International Airport-based company that specialises in both oil-industry work and sightseeing trips, offers city tours daily. At around Dhs3,000 for a 30-minute flight, they do not come cheap, although that this cost can be split between a maximum of four passengers.

Tours depart from the VIP Terminal at Dubai International Airport, which is located next to the Airport Expo, further along the highway from the main arrivals and departures terminal. Once inside, ask for Aerogulf Services or Executive Flight Services.

THE TOUR

The route for the 30-minute tour follows the Creek towards its mouth, with Deira (and highlights including Dubai Creek Golf & Yacht Club, Dubai Chamber of Commerce, National Bank of Dubai, Deira Old Souk, Al Ahmadiya School) to the right; and Bur Dubai and Shindagha

(Ruler's Court, Bastakiya, Al Fahidi Fortress, Dubai Old Souk, Sheikh Saeed Al Maktoum House) to the left.

Banking to the left at the Creek's mouth, you will have a bird's-eye view of Port Rashid, which handles some of the world's largest oil tankers, before flying along the Jumeira coast. Here, look out for landmarks such as Jumeira Mosque, Jumeira Beach Corniche and Jumeira Park.

The highlight of the trip, however, is probably seeing Burj Al Arab and the Palm Jumeirah from the sky – spectacular sights that help to justify the cost of the flight. On the trip back to the airport, there is still plenty to see, too, including Emirates Golf Club, the skyscrapers of Sheikh Zayed Road – notably the world's tallest building, Burj Dubai – and the camel racetrack at Nad Al Sheba.

Note that you can also arrange helicopter tours tailored to more specific needs through Aerogulf Services, such as flights over the desert to Hatta.

Above from far left: Aerogulf helicopter passing the Burj Al Arab; detail of one of the Palm's fronds, shot from above.

Below: Aerogulf helicopter above the Palm and the Burj Al Arab: the highlights of the tour.

DHOW CRUISE

One of the best ways of enjoying the Creek waterfront is to take an afternoon or evening dhow cruise, with lunch or dinner provided. Choose between an old-fashioned wooden dhow or a sleek modern catamaran.

What's In A Name?
The name 'dhow' comes from the Swahili word for boat, *dau.*

Abra Charters
An alternative to a dhow cruise is chartering an *abra* (*see top*) from any of Dubai's six *abra* stations; this costs around Dhs100 per hour. At the other end of the scale, look out for the plethora of state-of-the-art yachts in the Dubai area.

TIME 1–2 hours
START/END Dubai Creek
POINTS TO NOTE
Take a taxi from your hotel to the starting point for your dhow cruise on Dubai Creek (operators are based in various locations). Companies such as Net Tours (tel: 04 266 6655) and Tour Dubai (tel: 04 336 8407) can pick you up from your hotel. It is best to book your dhow cruise at least one day in advance to avoid disappointment.

If the sight of Dubai from the air *(see tour 5)* is a treat, views from the water should be mandatory. The city has welcomed seafarers throughout its history and the deck of a boat still offers a fine platform from which to observe onshore activities. A Creek cruise or an afternoon's sailing along the Gulf coast places you at both the centre of city life and its periphery. Time seems to slow down on such a journey, giving the voyager a rare opportunity for observation and reflection in this hyperactive city. Major landmarks you can expect to see en route include the National Bank of Dubai building, Dubai Chamber of Commerce, the Radisson SAS hotel on the Deira side and Sheikh Saeed Al Maktoum House, Beit Al Wakeel and the Shindagha Heritage area on the Bur Dubai side.

Wooden Dhows

Although a short ride on an *abra* water taxi *(see tours 1 and 4, pp.33 and 57)* is not to be missed, it is the traditional wooden dhow that offers the most authentic Creek experience. On the Bur Dubai side of the Creek, you will find dhows that have been built or adapted for tours behind the HSBC building. Net Tours (tel: 04 266 6655) operates daily dinner cruises from here between 8–10pm (hotel pick-ups can be arranged from 7pm).

Further up the Creek, near Al Garhoud Bridge, Al Boom Tourist Village (tel: 04 324 3000) is the biggest operator of dhows in Dubai. It runs lunch cruises on Fridays as well as two nightly dinner cruises from 8.30 to 10pm and 10.30pm to midnight.

On the Deira side of the Creek, tourist dhows are moored between the Radisson SAS Hotel Dubai Deira Creek and the Chamber of Commerce. The Radisson SAS's *Al Mansour Dhow* (tel: 04 222 7171) departs on two-hour dinner cruises at 8.30pm. One-hour sightseeing tours on the Tour Dubai Floating Majlis

(tel: 04 336 8407) depart at 11.30am, 1.30pm, 3.30pm and 5.30pm from the same area (no food on board, but drinks are provided).

MODERN ALTERNATIVE

Just as the skyline has changed, so too have some of the boats that ply the Creek. Modern alternatives to dhows (and *abras – see left*) include the luxurious 34-m (111-ft) Danat Dubai catamaran, run by Danat Dubai Cruises (tel: 04 351 1117). A scenic dinner cruise with an international buffet sails the Creek and open sea (weather permitting) between 8.30–11pm. The company also operates a traditional dhow cruise with an Arabic and international buffet from 8.15 to 10.15pm. Both options depart from the Bur Dubai creekside at the junction of Al Seef Road and Sheikh Khalifa Bin Zayed/Trade Centre Road.

Above from far left: all set for diners, on board a dhow; workman repairing a dhow.

Medieval Ships

Most Arabian seaman in pre-modern times spent days and nights exposed to the elements, in conditions of hardship and hard work. They would have made voyages in smallish vessels, the planks of which were not nailed but stitched together, a mode of shipbuilding that came as a constant surprise to Europeans and Arabs from the Mediterranean, such as Marco Polo and the North African explorer Ibn Battuta who had first-hand experience of them. Hull planks were stitched together edge-to-edge with coconut twine, and the ribs fitted later – the opposite of European boats. Gaps were caulked with a mixture of coir and fish oil being rammed into them. Except in larger vessels even a partial deck or a cabin was a luxury. Ships were still pointed at both ends, and used steering oars, one on each side. The square sail had evolved into something more triangular, enabling ships to sail close to the wind though not to tack in a modern sense. The boat was essentially a cargo-carrying tub which needed constant maintenance. Crew and passengers accommodated themselves as best they could on top of the cargo, and ablutions were carried out in a precarious box slung out over the side of the boat. The main advantage of such a craft was that it was flexible in heavy surf, and therefore less likely than more robustly built ships to be smashed while coming inshore. These fragile craft could be quite large, some carrying up to 400 men. At the height of Gulf trade, in the 9th century, Gulf seamen were sailing all the way to China in such ships, and there was a huge colony of Arab merchants at Canton. By sailing all the way like this Arab merchants could cut out the middleman and make massive profits. Gulf merchants' tales of the 8th–10th centuries describe hair-raising shipwrecks and adventures, and enormous mercantile risks. The loss of a single cargo could ruin a group of merchants and even contribute to the decline of a port. The rewards of a single successful voyage were correspondingly prodigious: a merchant could make his fortune for life.

DUBAILAND

Bigger than Disneyland and Disney World combined, bigger than four-and-a-half Manhattans, Dubailand is a vast entertainment complex and futuristic city rising in phases from the desert near Emirates Road.

DISTANCE 40km (25 miles) round trip

TIME A half or full day

START/END Central Dubai

POINTS TO NOTE

Dubailand covers a huge area around Emirates Road, so you will need a car to cover the whole development. For details of car-rental agencies, *see p.108*. For a single destination such as Dubai Polo Club take a taxi, but be sure to book your return journey.

Dubailand ❶ is very much a work in progress but it is such a vast new development within Dubai that it deserved to feature here. It will be 2018 before the last phase of this city within a city – comprising theme parks, thrill rides, hotels, spas, sports facilities and shopping malls – is complete, but even at this early stage there is still plenty to see. Some attractions are open to visitors already, but, extraordinarily, the scale of the building work itself is something that draws many people specifically to visit. However, if you are

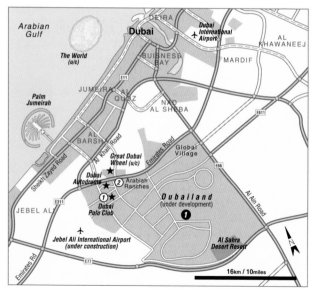

short of time and prefer a more finished attraction, it is probably worth waiting until the park is closer to completion before doing this tour.

DUBAILAND SIGHTS

To reach Dubailand, the best route out of central Dubai is south along Sheikh Zayed Road. Continue over the highway through Al Quoz and Al Barsha until you come to Arabian Ranches roundabout on Emirates Road (E311). Return the same way.

Some attractions have already opened to the public. These include the **Al Sahra Desert Resort**, a brand-new but nonetheless atmospheric heritage destination, off Exit 29 of the Dubai-Al Ain Road, where live shows are held in an open-air amphitheatre; the Andalusia-influenced **Dubai Polo Club** at the Arabian Ranches property development (**Palermo**, *see* ⑪①, is a great venue for brunch on Fridays between November and April, when polo matches are held; alternatively choose **Al Arrab**, *see* ⑪②, for a pitstop); **Dubai Autodrome**, a venue for racing events, go-karting and rock concerts; and the international pavilions of **Dubai Shopping Festival's Global Village** on Emirates Road, which is packed with visitors every year between December and February.

Futuristic Highlights

Among the more futuristic attractions that have yet to open are: the City of Arabia 'dinosaur entertainment city'; three theme parks at 'Legends'; a Las Vegas-style recreation of international landmarks at 'Falcon City of Wonders'; a snow dome; a polo and equestrian club, and the Aqua Dunya water park.

Above from far left: motorbike ride; note that Dubailand is a work in progress and much of the site is still under construction.

Below: advertisement for the new park.

Food and Drink 🍴

① PALERMO

Dubai Polo Club, Arabian Ranches; tel: 04 361 8111; daily noon–10.30pm; $$$
Spanish restaurant in a ranch-style venue overlooking green polo fields. Menu includes tapas plus mains such as steaks, pork ribs and lamb chops. Free sangria is offered with certain promotions (drivers: note Dubai's zero tolerance to drink-driving).

② AL ARRAB

Arabian Ranches Shopping Centre, off Emirates Road; tel: 04 361 7070; daily noon–midnight; $$–$$$
Lebanese restaurant offering mezze and grills. Other options within this shopping centre include the Black Canyon Thai café and Basta Art Café.

Experience
Dubailand

RAS AL KHOR
WILDLIFE SANCTUARY

Aimed at would-be ornithologists this tour involves a peaceful half a day's bird-spotting at Ras Al Khor Wildlife Sanctuary. Dubai's only nature reserve, the sanctuary is a magnet for flamingos and myriad other birds.

Above: heron at Ras Al Khor.

Above from top left: Dubai flamingos; patient spectating in a hide at the sanctuary.

Below: feeding time.

DISTANCE 10km (6 miles)
TIME Half a day
START Wafi City Mall
END Ras Al Khor Wildlife Sanctuary
POINTS TO NOTE
The sanctuary is closed on Fridays. Do not worry if you do not have binoculars with you – they are provided in the hide. For permits (for groups of 6 or more), contact the Marine and Sanctuaries Unit, Dubai Municipality, tel: 04 206 4240/60.

Dubai has become something of a birdwatcher's paradise, with up to 400 species in the country, around 90 of which are resident breeds. The UAE serves as a crossroads for north–south migrations from Europe to Africa and east–west migrations from India to the Near East. Up to 200 species, including bulbuls, doves, hoopoes, shrikes and wheatears, have been spotted at the Emirates Golf Club alone, while in the city, at the Dubai Creek Golf & Yacht Club *(see p.41)* you'll see parakeets, Indian rollers and little green bee-eaters. The city's flamingo population

can be found at the city's only nature reserve, the focus of this tour.

RAS AL KHOR

Ras Al Khor Wildlife Sanctuary ❶ (tel: 04 206 4240; Sat–Thur 9am–4pm; free but permits required for groups of 6 or more people – *see grey box left*) is at the southern end of the Creek. It can be reached from Wafi City Mall, home to **Carter's**, see ⑪①, our suggestion for a bite to eat before you settle down to some serious birdwatching.

From Wafi City Mall, head via Oud Metha Road/Route E66 towards Al Ain, then at the Bukudra Interchange near Nad Al Sheba Racecourse double back to the lay-by near one of the sanctuary's three wooden viewing hides. Leave your car in the lay-be parallel to the main road; the gate for pedestrian access to the hide is right there (you walk a further 100m/330ft or so after the gate to the hide itself, so that the traffic doesn't disturb the birds). Note that a second hide is located off Ras Al Khor Road as you approach Bukudra Interchange from Al Awir or Rashidiya.

Note that January is the overall best month to visit the sanctuary, and but recommended months for viewing migrating birds are October and March.

Statistics and Species

The sanctuary is a tidal lagoon that can host up to 15,000 birds on a single day, including between 1,000 and 1,500 migrant greater flamingos *(Phoenicopterus rubber)*, which have been a protected species here since 1985. The flamingos come to Dubai for the winter from lakes in northern Iran, and the government has tried to get them to breed here. The sanctuary also supports 30 per cent of all wading birds found in the UAE. Other than flamingos, species that might be spotted here include Socotra cormorants, cream-coloured coursers and crab plovers.

Dubai Zoo

If all this bird-watching puts you in the mood to see more wildlife, you could visit Dubai Zoo. Originally a refuge for animals illegally smuggled into Dubai, the zoo had long outgrown its old cramped Jumeira site, which was a cause of concern for animal lovers. A new site near Mushrif Park covers 108 ha (270 acres) and is designed along the lines of a state-of-the-art safari park. An educational facility as well as a tourist site, it has a camel safari, night zoo and botanical garden.

Food and Drink 🍴

① CARTER'S

Pyramids, Wafi City, Oud Metha; tel: 04 324 0000; daily 12.30pm–midnight; $$–$$$

Carter's is a modern, upscale version of a country pub, with great pub grub served by friendly waiting staff, with a live band in the background. During the cooler months, the alfresco seating is popular, so reservation is recommended.

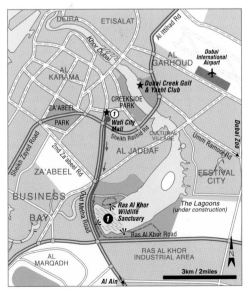

9

RACE NIGHT AT NAD AL SHEBA

The prospect of an evening at the races on the edge of the Arabian desert is loaded with romantic possibilities. Access to the grandstands is free; alternatively, pay the (very affordable) day-member's fee at the Nad Al Sheba Club and watch from the balcony of a members' box high in the grandstand.

TIME Nov–Apr, from 7pm (from 9pm during Ramadan)
START/END Nad Al Sheba
POINTS TO NOTE
Take a taxi from your hotel to the racecourse or follow the instructions in the grey box for route 3 *(see p.42)*. The races begin at 7pm and are held every half hour thereafter, except in the month of Ramadan, when they begin at 9pm. Visit the website www.emiratesracing.com for further information.

You do not have to dress up and experience corporate-style hospitality to enjoy a night at **Nad Al Sheba Racecourse ❶**. Unlike most events in Dubai, admission is free throughout the November–April race season and with it comes unlimited access to most areas, including the lower seating of the two grandstands and the area around the parade ring. Consequently, there is a unique multicultural atmosphere during each meeting, and it is being in the thick of this – rather than above it – that makes an evening at the races here so enjoyable. Recommendations

Below: watching the floodlit races.

for eating at the racecourse include **Links**, see 🍴①. (For dining outside the course, try **The Agency**, see 🍴②.)

NAD AL SHEBA

The racecourse attracts a mixture of nationalities, with members of the East African communities, who love racing, particularly prominent. Walk around the floodlit venue between each of the evening's six or seven races and you will pass men, women and children sitting on blankets spread over the grass, playing cards, picnicking and generally making the evening a family outing.

Royal Attendance

Racing may no longer be the sport of European kings – Queen Elizabeth II notwithstanding – but it is emphatically the sport of Arab sheikhs. A race night

at Nad Al Sheba offers you the best chance of seeing members of Dubai's ruling family up close. Sheikh Mohammed Bin Rashid Al Maktoum, vice president and prime minister of the UAE and ruler of Dubai, is a familiar figure in the royal box (in the centre of the smaller grandstand) and paddock. Sheikh Mohammed is well known to horse racing aficionados as the supremo behind the Godolphin stable.

Practicalities

Gambling is illegal in Dubai, but if you fancy a flutter, the Pick Six competition offers a cash prize to anyone who guesses all six (or seven) of the winning horses in that evening's races. The Pick Six forms are available on entry and are as simple to complete as a lottery form; they must be submitted at least 15 minutes before the first race.

Above from far left: the swish set at the races; speeding to the finish.

International Village

If you are in Dubai during the last week of March, pay the entrance fee for the International Village at the Dubai World Cup (book on www.dubai worldcup.com). This, the highlight of Dubai's social calendar, attracts crowds of up to 70,000, often including such celebrity race fans as Imran Khan, Rod Stewart and Bo Derek. With prize money of $21.25 million, it is the richest horse race in the world.

Food and Drink 🍴

① LINKS TERRACE
Nad Al Sheba Club, adjacent to racecourse; tel: 04 336 3666; daily 7–11pm; $$–$$$
The best thing about this restaurant is that you can dine without missing the action on the racecourse. Be sure to have a reservation if you plan on going on a race night.

② THE AGENCY
Jumeirah Emirates Towers, Sheikh Zayed Road; tel: 04 330 0000; Sun–Thur noon–midnight, Fri–Sat 3pm–3am; $$
A tapas bar offering a good wine selection and located not far from the racecourse where the swish set of Dubai like to be seen.

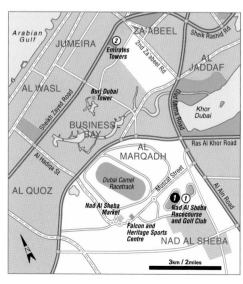

MOSQUE VISIT AND CULTURAL LUNCH

Sample local life and help build bridges between cultures by taking part in tours and events organised by the Sheikh Mohammed Centre for Cultural Understanding in Bur Dubai's Bastakiya district.

Dress Appropriately
In addition to dressing appropriately *(see grey box, right)* before entering the mosque, you will be required to remove your shoes and enter in your bare or stocking feet, as is the custom. You should also remove your shoes at the Cultural Centre.

TIME Allow 1½ hrs per activity
START/END Sheikh Mohammed Centre for Cultural Understanding or Jumeira Mosque
POINTS TO NOTE
Do this route on a Sunday if you want to attend the mosque visit and the cultural lunch; an alternative is to do the walking tour, then the lunch. Visitors to the mosque should ensure they are appropriately dressed, with arms and legs covered (plus headscarves for women). Children under the age of five are not allowed into the mosque.

About 80 per cent of the UAE's population of over 5 million are expatriates, so it is quite possible to visit Dubai and leave without having met a single UAE national or, indeed, a Gulf Arab (excluding airport and post office workers).

CULTURAL CENTRE

However, you are sure to meet locals if you visit the **Sheikh Mohammed Centre for Cultural Understanding** ❶ (tel: 04 353 6666; www.cultures.ae; Sun–Thur 8am–3pm, Sat 9am–noon; free except tours and lunch), a non-profit-making organisation, established

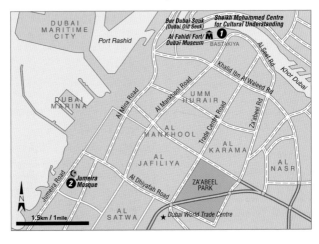

by and named after Dubai's ruler, which aims to promote mutual understanding and acceptance among people from different cultures.

To reach the centre, go along Al Seef Road, heading away from the Al Maktoum Bridge, towards the Dubai Museum. At the end of Al Seef Road, turn left at the roundabout for Bastakiya, then first right for the centre, which has a car park. The centre is housed in a renovated wind-tower.

JUMEIRA MOSQUE VISIT

The centre organises visits to the **Jumeira Mosque ❷** (Sat, Sun, Tue and Thur 10am; meet at the mosque), currently the only way for non-Muslims to enter the building. There is no need to book, but you should meet at the mosque itself and register just outside. At the end of the tour is an illuminating talk on culture in the UAE and Islam, followed by a question-and-answer session.

WALKING TOUR

The Sheikh Mohammed Centre also organises guided walking tours (Sat–Sun, Tue, Thur 10am; booking on telephone number above left essential; charge) of the Bastakiya district in which it is located; these last approximately one and a half hours and give you the background on the architecture and heritage of this area. You may choose them as a complement – or an alternative – to tour 4 *(see pp.52–9)* in this guidebook.

CULTURAL LUNCH

In its bid to support 'Free exchanges of ideas about Dubai, its people and its culture', the centre organises a cultural lunch (Sun 1pm; booking on above telephone number essential; charge) as well as a cultural breakfast (Mon 10am; booking essential; charge) of homemade traditional Emirati food *(see p.15)*. Both provide insight into a culture that is usually poorly represented in the Western media. It is best to do the mosque tour, followed by the Sunday lunch. While you are at the centre, take time to explore its heritage shop, which sells local handmade gifts.

Above from far left: the domes of Jumeira Mosque; devotees at prayer.

Religious Tolerance

According to the Sheikh Mohammed Centre for Cultural Understanding, 'Cultural and religious diversity has made the Emirates probably the most open and tolerant country within the region. Dubai and the UAE in general are liberal in allowing foreigners to maintain their own religious practices and lifestyles.' Although Emiratis are Muslims, and the legal system that applies to locals and foreigners alike is based on Islamic Sharia law, the Dubai Government allows people of other faiths to gather for worship, as long as they do not prose-lytise Muslims. A number of Christian churches have been established on land provided by the rulers on the Bur Dubai side of the Creek. As Friday is the local weekend, most churches have main services then – Sunday is a normal working day.

Sand Dunes
كثبان رملية

DESERT ADVENTURE

Forget the Creek, forget the beaches, forget the shopping: if you have not spent at least a few hours in the desert you have not truly experienced Dubai. No visit to the city is complete without a trip into the timeless sands, and for most people this is best done through an official tour company.

Above: desert blooms; local hazard.

Below: spectacular sand dunes.

DISTANCE 150km (93 miles) round trip
TIME A half or full day
START/END Central Dubai
POINTS TO NOTE

By rental car you can see and photograph the Arabian desert from the Dubai-Hatta and Sharjah-Dhaid roads, but if you want to venture into the dunes, for safety book a four-wheel-drive safari with a licensed tour operator. We do not recommend restaurants en route for obvious reasons – there aren't many – so remember to take plenty of water and snacks to keep you going.

For all its striking modernity, Dubai is built on sand and the desert way of life, and explorations of the dunes and dry river beds *(wadis)* in the outlying emirate will help you better understand the city and its people. If that seems too worthy a reason, the desert can be stunningly beautiful and, of course, tremendous fun – speeding over the dunes in a luxury 4x4 with an expert driver can be thoroughly exhilarating.

Around 65 per cent of the 85,000 sq km (33,000 sq miles) of the UAE is desert. The term encompasses a variety of landscapes and conditions: as well as rolling dunes, it includes salt flats *(sabkha)*, flood plains, mountains and river valleys. The desert that begins on the outskirts of Dubai (or more accurately within the city limits, where every vacant lot is sandy) forms part of the Saharo-Arabian Desert, the most extensive dry zone in the world. It is possible to enter via **Al Awir**, on the city limits, and see nothing but desert until you tap the sand from your shoes near the Syria-Lebanon border thousands of kilometres away.

THE LARGEST DUNES

You do not need to travel so far to gauge the desert's vastness. The nearest

large dunes to Dubai are found at **Qarn Nazwa** ❶ on the Dubai–Hatta road, beginning about 15km (9 miles) beyond Lahbab roundabout. These dunes offer a glimpse of the stereotypical desert landscape, and if you have a rental car you do not have to join a specialist tour to see them from the safety of the highway. Be aware that this is a popular area for dune driving, however, with several quad-bike rental companies on either side of the road. If you are hoping for a photograph of virgin desert or craving solitude and silence, you may be disappointed.

Desert Landscape

Heading inland on the highway from the Dubai coast towards Qarn Nazwa, you first pass through terrain known as *sabkha* – formed over the course of 7,000 years by wind erosion and tides – followed by a landscape of scrubby sand. (You might be surprised by the desert's greenness; residents say it is becoming greener by the year.) You then encounter barren rolling dunes tinted red by deposits of iron oxide; if you stop to run the sand through your fingers, it seems to be mixed with paprika.

Desert Tour

The desert can be a deadly environment for the inexperienced and ill-prepared, so do not even think about venturing off-road in a rental 4x4 unless you are with a local expert and a second vehicle. By far the best way to explore the desert is with one of Dubai's numerous specialist tour companies; exact routes vary from company to company, but all tend to include camel farms, Bedouin villages and roller-coaster dune rides. Your guide should fill you in on the Bedouin way of life and desert ecology, as well as identifying plants and any animal tracks you might find in the sand.

Arabian Adventures (tel: 04 343 9966; www.arabian-adventures.com), Net Tours (tel: 04 266 6655) and Orient Tours (tel: 06 568 2323; www. orient

Above from far left: 4x4 on the road; watch out for sand dunes; vegetation for the dry climate; hot-air ballooning offers a spectacular way of viewing the desert.

Be Prepared
Although it's generally not as humid as the coast, the desert is, of course, extremely hot during the day. So make sure you pack plenty of liquid refreshments, sun cream and a hat for your desert safari. And if you are going to be out there after sunset, pack a jumper – without cloud cover to trap the heat of the day, Arabian nights can be very chilly.

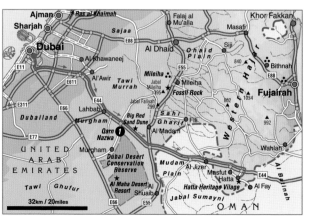

Above from left: desert walk; Hatta Heritage Village viewed from its defensive watchtower.

tours.ae) are among several well-established companies offering half- or full-day forays into the desert, with hotel pick-ups. For an off-road adventure with a twist, consider The Hummer Adventures by 7 Tours (tel: 04 397 9809; www.7tours.ae), which operates a fleet of Hummer H2 vehicles.

Your hotel should have information on specialist tours and may even run its own programme for guests. For example, the Hatta Fort Hotel *(see p.76)* has an excellent tour to Fossil Rock, so called because of the marine-life fossils that can be found there, while the luxury Al Maha Desert Resort & Spa,

Arabia's first eco-tourism resort, offers a wildlife drive through the 225-sq-km (87-sq-mile) conservation reserve in which it is located.

Fossil Rock and Big Red

If possible, opt for a tour that visits dunes and *wadis*, ideally Fossil Rock and Big Red, both of which are popular with locals and expat residents. Another favourite is **Wadi Bih** – further afield but manageable in a day trip that follows a rugged route from Ras al Khaimah through the canyons, gorges and terraced hillsides of the 1,200-m (4,000-ft) Hajar Mountains.

Above: long, empty road; desert scene.

'Unicorns'

If your organised desert tour takes you through the Dubai Desert Conservation Reserve, look out for Arabian oryx, a rare antelope-like animal that has been brought back from the edge of extinction in the 1970s. Because its two horns look like a single horn in profile, the Arabian oryx is believed to have given rise to the unicorn myth.

When to Visit the Desert

The best time to experience the desert is late afternoon, when the light is as soft and warm as the sand underfoot. You might opt for a desert dinner tour (4–10pm), during which you will see the sunset and a night sky that, away from any ambient light, is remarkably clear. Alternatively, if you take an overnight trip, departing Dubai around 4pm, you will see the sunset and, after a night watching shooting stars, sunrise. If you are prepared to forego the comfort of a luxury 4x4 in your search for excitement, contact Desert Rangers (tel: 04 340 2408; www.desertrangers.com), which organises activities such as sandboarding and dune-buggy safaris.

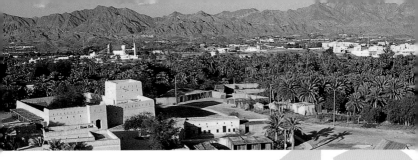

HATTA

This is a one- or two-day trip into the Hajar Mountains and Hatta, with its fort and springs. Avoid going on Fridays and public holidays, when the track to Hatta Pools is clogged with 4x4s and other vehicles from the city. If you want to stay overnight, the Hatta Fort Hotel is recommended.

Hatta ❶, an enclave of Dubai, is surrounded by territory belonging to Oman, Ras Al Khaimah and Ajman, but visitors do not need passports or visas to enter the area and there are no checkpoints to pass through. The border post for Oman is actually 10km (6 miles) further to the east of Hatta.

To reach Hatta from central Dubai, take route 44. The first sign that you are nearing Hatta is the sight of roadside carpet stalls, followed by the hilltop summer homes that belong to Dubai's sheikhs and wealthy businessmen. When you reach the roundabout with an open-sided fortress in the middle, either turn left for the gateway to the Hatta Fort Hotel, or turn right for Hatta Heritage Village and the road to Hatta Pools.

HERITAGE VILLAGE

Hatta Heritage Village ❷ (tel: 04 851 1374; Sat–Thur 8.30am–8.30pm, Fri 3pm–8.30pm; free) brings the community's colourful history to life. Various styles of mountain dwellings have been rebuilt around carefully restored buildings, including the first fort in the emirate of Dubai, constructed in 1790, which now houses a weaponry museum. Check out the

DISTANCE 250km (155 miles) round trip
TIME A full day or overnight
START/END Hatta
POINTS TO NOTE
The no. 16 bus runs between Dubai and Hatta (daily 6am–10pm; leaves hourly from Al Sabkha Bus Station, Deira). To explore the surrounding area, however, you should rent a car (see p.108).

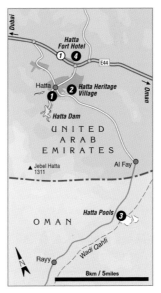

Above: pot seller in Hatta; old well.

Arabian Leopard
The Hajar Mountains are the habitat of the rare Arabian Leopard, known locally as *nimr*. Smaller and lighter in colour than its African counterpart, the Arabian leopard is a nocturnal hunter and seldom seen. It is estimated there are fewer than 100 in the wild, and six to ten of them in the UAE. A captive male and female, 'Arnold' and 'Lucy', are part of a breeding programme at Sharjah Natural History Museum and Desert Park.

Above from left: *wadi* in the Hajar Mountains; restful spot on the coast. **Below:** watchtower near Hatta; beware of dry river beds; towards Hatta.

Prehistoric Hatta
Archaeology reveals that the fertile mountain valleys around Hatta were inhabited more than 4,000 years ago, during the Bronze Age. Excavations in the Juma valley have uncovered an ancient settlement and tombs similar to those found in Umm Al Nar, Abu Dhabi, dating from c.2,000–2,500BC. Finds from the site are displayed at Dubai Museum (see p.30).

fascinating variety of mud and *barasti* (palm frond) houses and a restored *falaj* irrigation system that channels water through the village to the neighbourhood's date-palm gardens. On weekends and public holidays, local women in national dress and *burqa* face masks work away at traditional crafts and will pose for photographs, if you want them, though, importantly, ask their permission first. The watchtowers that loom high over the village date back to 1850.

HATTA POOLS

The heritage village aside, Hatta's main attraction for many are the **Hatta Pools ❸** and the off-road drive that continues beyond the pools through Wadi Qahfi to the Omani village of Rayy. The dirt track that leads to the pools begins several kilometres/miles from Hatta itself. The Hatta Fort Hotel *(see right)* can provide navigation sheets with directions and key landmarks to guests who have their own 4x4s. Alternatively, you might book a tour in a 4x4 through the hotel to share the expense of vehicle and driver with other guests.

The Pools

Don't expect idyllic pools, cascading waterfalls and a brimming river at Hatta Pools and you won't be disappointed. The stunning but parched landscape around the pools bears comparison with the surface of Mars. The access track is dusty, the river bed largely dry, while the spring pools are

made up of low-level, slow-moving water. Throughout the year, there is enough water at crossing points to make a splash though.

HATTA FORT HOTEL

Some would claim that Hatta's best attraction is the **Hatta Fort Hotel ❹** (PO Box 9277, Hatta; tel: 04 852 3211; www.hattaforthotel.com; *see p.115*) itself, a venerable institution surrounded by dry, jagged, volcanic rock. Its 50 rooms have a safari-lodge feel and open onto a spectacular vista of the distant village, mountains and sky.

Even if you are not planning to stay the night, you can lunch at **Gazebo**, *see* 🍴①, or, for a nominal charge, relax by the pool. You could also try your hand at clay-pigeon shooting or archery in the hotel's grounds.

BACK TO DUBAI

To get back to Dubai, return to Hatta, then pick up route 44, which leads all the way back.

Food and Drink 🍴

① GAZEBO
Hatta Fort Hotel, Hatta; tel: 04 852 3211; daily 11am–7pm; $$–$$$
Located on an air-conditioned balcony above the famous hotel's gorgeous swimming pool, Gazebo offers a marvellous view of the landscaped gardens and the rugged Hajar mountains beyond. The menu offers a range of international dishes. and the service is usually very friendly.

THE NORTHERN EMIRATES

The drive from Dubai through the northern emirates of Sharjah, Ajman and Umm al Qaiwain is like a journey back in time: the further you travel, the more you can envisage how Dubai looked before the oil boom.

The northern emirates extend to Ras al Khaimah, some 140km (87 miles) from Dubai, but with so much to see, the last stop on this car-based day trip is in Umm al Qaiwain. As you head northeast, away from Dubai, you pass through a less-wealthy, less-populous and less-developed UAE. At Umm al Qaiwain, with a population of only

DISTANCE 162km (100 miles) round trip

TIME A full day

START/END Dubai

POINTS TO NOTE

A rental car *(see p.108)* is required for this itinerary. The most interesting route north follows the coastal roads through Sharjah, Ajman and Umm al Qaiwain, with the Arabian Gulf on your left. For a quicker journey, consider the inland Emirates Road (E311). The ideal is a combination of coast road out and E311 back.

Eastern Sharjah
References to 'Sharjah', which means 'eastern' in Arabic, date to at least 1490, when the Arab navigator Ahmad Ibn Majid wrote that ships could find this area if they followed the stars from the island of Tunb.

Below: boats viewed from Sharjah Bridge.

Centre for the Arts
Following the establishment of Sharjah Art Museum in 1995, the emirate has developed a reputation as a centre for the arts in the UAE. The eighth Sharjah Biennial, a two-month show featuring work by international artists, was held in 2007 at various venues, including the Expo Centre and the waterfront Qanat Al Qasba cultural area.

75,000, you may feel as though you have travelled back in time to the modest pre-oil days.

You could spend a day in any one of the emirates mentioned here – what follows is less of a one-day itinerary than an overview of the route with our suggestions. If you leave Dubai at 9am and allow for around three hours in Sharjah, an hour or so in Ajman and two and a half hours in Umm al Qaiwain, you should have an enjoyable and varied day.

SHARJAH

Roads to **Sharjah ❶**, the UAE's third-largest emirate after Abu Dhabi and Dubai (population 750,000), are well signposted, but as you near the city it

is very easy to get lost in its outlying industrial areas. The traditional – and most direct – route from Dubai to areas of interest in Sharjah is the E11 highway, which becomes Al Ittihad Road where it passes the west boundary fence of Dubai International Airport.

The highway, which can be clogged with bumper-to-bumper traffic in rush hour, passes Dubai Police Headquarters and Al Mulla Plaza before entering Sharjah. Exit either at Interchange 1 or the next interchange, following the brown signs for the 'Heritage Area'. Alternatively, you could take the E311 Emirates Road, which passes east – inland – of Dubai airport and Al Qusais. Again, look out for brown signs directing you to the 'Heritage Area'.

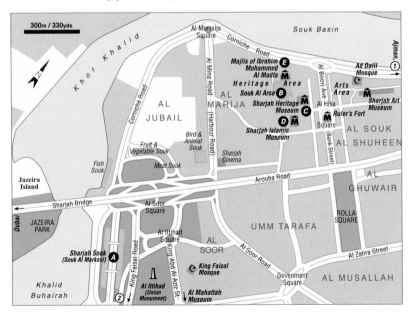

Towards the Souk

Arouba Road is the most attractive entrance to a city that was named cultural capital of the Arab world by Unesco in 1998. (Until alcohol was banned in Sharjah in 1985, it had a more promising future as a tourist destination than Dubai.) As the road rises to cross Khalid Creek at Sharjah Bridge, you can see Port Khalid – the huge metal frames are oil rigs due for repairs – and dhows around the Fish Souk.

To the right, the 10-sq-km (4-sq-mile) Jazeira Park occupies its own island. Beyond this, the 100-m (330-ft) high fountain at **Khalid Lagoon** is the third highest in the world, after those in Geneva and Jeddah.

A little further on, **Sharjah Souk Ⓐ** *(see box below)* can be seen on the right, along with the gold-topped Al Ittihad ('Union') Monument and the **King Faisal Mosque**, which towers over the verdant Al Ittihad Square.

Above from far left: Sharjah corniche by night; historic building; King Faisal Mosque.

Sharjah Markets
On the opposite side of the flyover from Sharjah's souk, there are markets specialising in fish, fruit and vegetables, and animals.

Sharjah Souk

To most Dubai residents it is known simply as Sharjah Souk (Sat–Thur 9am–1pm and 4–10pm, closed Fri am), a treasure trove of carpets, antique furniture and Gulf mementos; it is also called Sharjah New Souk, Blue Souk, Central Souk and Souk Al Markasi. Nothing in Dubai comes close to it in size, content or atmosphere. Some of the big shopping centres have air-conditioned shops that sell similar goods, but the choice is not as wide, nor is the bargaining experience an option; even Dubai's traditional old souks do not have the concentration of products available in Sharjah. The souk consists of two long parallel buildings split by a road but joined by overhead walkways. The attractive exterior features blue tiles, decorative windows and large wind-towers. The rounded roof has been likened to oil barrels lying side by side. Inside, the shops are on two levels. Unless you want perfume, cheap shoes, small electrical goods or audio tapes that are best found elsewhere, do not waste much time on the ground floor. Head straight to the upstairs antique and carpet shops.

Above: Al Mahattah Museum and exhibits.

The ruler of Sharjah is Dr Sheikh Sultan Bin Mohammed Al Qasimi, the only ruler of a UAE emirate to have earned a PhD. His thesis at Britain's Exeter University was on the 'myth' of piracy in the Arabian Gulf in the 18th and 19th centuries.

Below: Souq Al Majarra, Corniche Road, Sharjah.

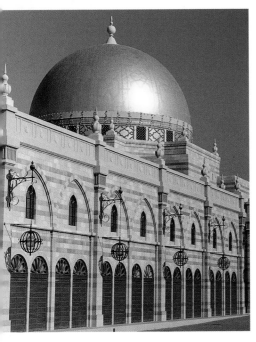

South-east of the souk is a good option for food, **Danial**, *ee* 🍴①.

Al Mahattah Museum

Beyond this point a man-made grassy knoll with a flower-bed urging passers-by to 'Smile, You Are In Sharjah', you can see King Abd Al Aziz Street leading towards the newer neighbourhoods. Until 1976, this street formed the main runway of the UAE's first airport. Originally established in 1932 as a stopover for British Imperial Airways flights from London to Australia, the airport was also a British Royal Air Force base and home to the Trucial Oman Scouts. The UAE's first hotel, the Fortress Hotel just off King Abd Al Aziz Street, has been restored and, with an air-traffic control tower, forms the aviation-themed **Al Mahattah Museum** (Immigration Road; tel: 06 573 3079; Tue–Thur and Sat–Sun 9am–1pm and 5–8pm, Fri 4–8pm; charge). Among the aircraft on display are a World War II-era Avro Anson and a Douglas DC3, which belonged to the Gulf Aviation Co., the forerunner of Gulf Air.

Take the right slip road immediately after Sharjah Bridge. If you want to visit the **Sharjah Souk** *(see box p.79)* or the aviation museum, carefully cross several lanes of traffic towards a road that cuts through the park and navigate your way from there.

Al Mina Road

After the souk or the museum, get back on to the slip road from Sharjah Bridge and continue as far as you can, following the road left underneath a flyover and then turning right onto Al Mina Road. You are on the right road, if Sharjah Cinema is immediately to your right. The bird-and-animal souk, where falcons are sold, is on a parallel street to the left.

Along the Corniche

Continue to a small roundabout at the Creek and turn right onto Corniche Road, along one side of which are moored numerous dhows. You will continue along this road towards Ajman later, but first park the car and take time to explore the **Heritage Area** that has been restored on either side of Al Boorj Avenue (aka Bank Street): it conveys a sense of life in the days

when Sharjah was a more important Gulf trading centre than Dubai.

Souk Al Arsa

Souk Al Arsa (Sat–Thur 9am–1pm and 4.30–9pm, Fri 4.30–9pm), the UAE's oldest souk, is set a little off Corniche Road before Bank Street in an enchanting neighbourhood of alleyways, minarets and wind-towers. Built with coral, limestone and plaster, and shaded by a palm-frond roof, the souk is full of antiques shops and stalls that sell everything from handicrafts and trinkets to honey and tobacco. Its friendly coffee shop is popular with elderly locals.

Heritage Museums

There are several museums in the area, including **Sharjah Heritage Museum** (tel: 06 566 5466; Tue–Thur, Sat 9am–1pm and 5–8pm, Fri and Sun 5–8pm; charge) in the former home of the Al Naboodah trading family. A tour of its colourful displays of regional costumes, jewellery and restored bedrooms is invariably followed by an invitation to recline on Bedu cushions and enjoy a fragrant cardamom-flavoured coffee with one of the guides.

Sharjah Islamic Museum (tel: 06 568 3334; www.uaeinteract.com/culture; Tue–Thur, Sat–Sun 8am–8pm, Fri 4–8pm; charge) is housed in the former residence of one Said bin Mohammed Al Shamsi. Do not expect to find out much about religion here, though: the museum is mainly a showcase for artefacts from Islamic countries.

Another attraction is the **Majlis of Ibrahim Mohammed Al Madfa** (tel: 06 568 1738; Sat–Thur 8am–8pm, Fri 4–8pm; free), heritage home of the founder of the region's first newspaper in 1927 and at one time an adviser to the ruling Al Qasimi family. The *majlis'* distinctive round wind-tower is the only one of its kind in the UAE. The building, where the magnate once received business guests, is now used to house a small museum, showcasing a number of his personal effects.

Ruler's Fort

The **Ruler's Fort** (tel: 06 568 5500; Tue–Thur, Sat–Sun 9am–1pm and 4–8pm, Fri 4–8pm; charge) is located in the middle of Bank Street, standing on what has become a large traffic island in a small canyon of banks and offices. An extension of the Heritage Area that includes the imposing purpose-built **Sharjah Art Museum** (tel: 06 822 2568; Tue–Thur, Sat 9am–1pm and 5–8pm, Fri and Sun 5–8pm; charge) and the venerable **Ad Dalil Mosque**, fronts onto the Corniche Road on the other side of Bank Street.

To Ajman

Back in your car, continue past the large Gulf-facing Radisson SAS Hotel on your left (home to the **Chillout**

Above from far left: Sharjah's waterfront, dominated by contemporary buildings; a bird's-eye view of the Heritage Area and Souq Al Arsa.

Food and Drink

① DANIAL

Crystal Plaza Mall, Buheirah Corniche, Sharjah; tel: 06 574 4668; daily 12.30pm–1.30am; $
Iranian restaurant serving good-value buffet meals. During the cooler months, it's a great place from which to enjoy the view of nearby Sharjah Souk and Khalid Lagoon – try to get a seat on the balcony for the views, if possible.

Café, *see* ①②, if you are hungry) and along a regal avenue of palm trees, wrought-iron railings and a showcase fountain that indicates that the modern Ruler's Palace is on your left.

At each of a succession of small roundabouts, bear left, and keep hugging the coast road. With its pristine, white-sand beach, this area is like a less developed version of Dubai's Jumeira coastline. You are now passing through the Sharjah suburbs into Ajman.

AJMAN

In terms of ambience, **Ajman** ❷ is much like the Dubai of the 1980s. The smallest of the UAE's seven emirates (250 sq km, 97 sq miles; population 275,000), Ajman has no oil wealth and continues to rely on traditional industries such as boat-building and fishing.

Ajman Museum

Its main attraction is the excellent **Ajman Museum** (tel: 06 742 3824; Sat–Thur 9am–1pm and 4–7pm, Fri 4–7pm; charge) in the town's old fort. To reach the museum, take a right turn at the Ajman Beach Hotel and follow the road alongside the edge of the pretty marina to Leewara Street. Turn right and, at the first roundabout, bear left towards Clocktower roundabout and Central Square. The fort will be to your left.

Below: a family stroll through Ajman.

Built *c.*1775, the fort was the ruler's official residence until 1970 and Ajman's police station in the 1970s. More appealing in some ways than its Dubai equivalent (the quieter, more parochial setting helps), the museum has a fine example of a wind-tower, which, unlike those in some other UAE museums, is fully functioning.

The museum showcases life in the region from ancient times to the modern era, with *barasti* houses and dhows just beyond the entrance and, in the old fort proper, displays on policing (practised since the days of the Prophet Mohammed in the 7th century), the bedroom of Sheikh Rashid bin Humaid Al Nuaimi (1928–81) and a market tableau.

For a good stopping point in Ajman, try **Café Kranzler**, see ①③.

UMM AL QAIWAIN

To continue to the emirate of **Umm al Qaiwain** ❸, pass through Ajman along Hamid Bin Abdul Aziz Street. At the first roundabout head for Al Ittihad Street at 11 o'clock. Continue until this street joins Badr Street and turn left. You are now on the road to Umm al Qaiwain. (If in doubt, follow signs for Ras al Khaimah.) The road from Ajman to Umm al Qaiwain passes through the first *sabkha* (salt flat) desert since leaving Dubai. Umm al Qaiwain basks on its own headland well off the main road linking Dubai with Ras al Khaimah; it is about halfway between the two and is well signposted.

Old Town

The old town is built on little more than a sandy spit at the tip of the headland. Approaching it along King Faisal Road, you might not realise that you are actually passing through the heart of the modern capital of an emirate, albeit the UAE's second-smallest. Umm al Qaiwain is so quiet that it is quite possible you will not see anyone on the streets until you reach the old town, and even then you are likely to see more goats than people. Other than the occasional Mercedes and

Above from far left: traditional dwellings and mosque tower in the heritage area of Sharjah; strolling along the beach at Ajman; Ajman Museum.

Above: Ajman Museum's wind-tower.

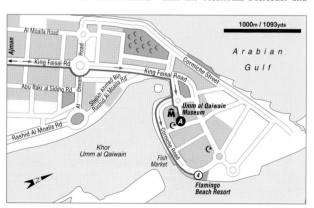

The *dugong* (manatee) population of the Arabian Gulf is thought to be the second largest in the world after Australia, and a significant number live in the waters off Umm al Qaiwain, where sea grass is plentiful. The world's oldest fossilised remains of a *dugong*, dating back 6,000 years, were found here, on Akab Island. It is believed sightings of this mammal by ancient sailors gave rise to the mermaid myth.

Below: aerial view of housing and a mosque in Umm al Qaiwain.

BMW, the odd battered old Land Rover or antiquated Indian Padmini, the roads are virtually free of traffic.

Three ancient watchtowers, once part of a fortified defensive wall, mark the boundary of the old town at the narrowest part of the headland, where King Faisal Road meets Al Soor Street. At this point you will see the old town away to your right across an enormous lagoon. On part of the lagoon's shoreline you will find one of Umm al Quwain's most appealing attractions – a forest of mangrove trees.

Umm al Quwain Museum

Take the first right and follow the road past a small public park. The town's old fortress – which, much like the one in Ajman, served as the residence of the local ruler in the years before it became a police station – stands in a small square

beyond the roundabout ahead and is now **Umm al Qaiwain Museum** Ⓐ (no tel: Sat–Sun, Tue–Thur 8am–1pm and 5–8pm, Fri 5–8pm; charge). In addition to the renovated fort itself, the museum showcases items found at nearby archaeological sites including Ad-Dour *(see opposite)* and sheds light on the history of the local area.

Flamingo Beach Resort

Take a right at the roundabout and follow Corniche Road past the fish market, where you are likely to see fishermen mending broken nets. Just before the road arcs left to continue its loop through the old town (before rejoining King Faisal Road), turn right into the **Flamingo Beach Resort**. Park the car and continue your exploration of the area by boat, which you can hire here by booking in advance.

ISLANDS OFF THE COAST

The islands that dot the Umm al Qaiwain coast – the largest of which is **As Siniyyah** ❹ – are the habitat of herons, cormorants, flamingos, turtles and even *dugong* (manatees or sea cows), which sailors of old mistook for mermaids *(see left)*. A motor-boat tour from the Flamingo Beach Resort costs Dhs180 per hour for a maximum of 15 people (last trip at 3pm). The best way to minimise the disturbance to wildlife is to ask the driver to cut the engine and let the boat drift in silence.

Afterwards, you might like to finish the day with sundowners at the resort's licensed bar, see 🍴④, but remember the zero-tolerance rule for alcohol if you're driving.

Dreamland Aqua Park

Alternatively, you might squeeze in a visit to **Dreamland Aqua Park** ❺ (tel: 06 768 1888; www.dreamlanduae.com; Jan–Mar: daily 10am–6pm, Apr–May: daily 10am–7pm, June–Aug: Sat–Thur 11am–9pm, Fri 10am–10pm, Sept–Dec: daily 10am–6pm; during Ramadan: 10am–4pm; charge), north of Umm al Qaiwain, on the highway to Ras al Khaimah. The park, which claims to be the world's largest, has 25 water rides and a go-kart track. There is also a restaurant here, see 🍴⑤.

Ad-Dour Archaeological Site

History enthusiasts might prefer a more highbrow sunset stroll through the low stone ruins of **Ad-Dour** ❻, an archaeological site to the right of the Ras al Khaimah highway as you head towards Dreamland, opposite Khor al Beidah. The largest pre-Islamic site on the Arabian Gulf, Ad-Dour, which means 'the houses' in Arabic, would have been a major trading centre in the Hellenistic era, from *c*.300BC to a century after the time of Christ. Finds here include Greek pottery. Ad-Dour is a candidate for the great city of Omana, the Dubai of its day, which was known to Classical geographers including Strabo and Pliny the Elder (*c*.23–79AD).

BACK TO DUBAI

For the return journey to Dubai, either go back the way you came – a route that can be clogged with traffic in the evening rush hour – or follow the signs to Emirates Road (E311), which bypasses much of the coastal cities' congested roads, though this can also be busy. Allow at least an hour and a half for your return journey.

Food and Drink

④ FLAMINGO BEACH RESORT
P.O.B. #1129, Umm al Qaiwain; tel: 06 765 0000; www.flamingoresort.ae; $$
There are limited options for eating out on this tour, but this pleasant coastal resort in the old town does food until 10pm. The Flamingo Café and tropical-style Beach Bar offer food such as seafood and multi-ethnic food in a relaxed setting. Dhow buffets, dinner buffets served in a dhow by the beach, are also organised. Alcoholic drinks are plentiful here.

⑤ DREAMLAND AQUA PARK
Umm al Qaiwain–Ras al Khaimah Road; tel: 06 768 1888; www.dreamlanduae.com; for times, see main entry, left; $$
There are five places to eat, plus a kiosk, at this huge water park, with cuisines ranging from pizza to Indian food. The relaxing poolside bar is the largest in the UAE. Alcohol served.

FUJAIRAH AND THE ARABIAN SEA

Hemmed in by the Hajar Mountains, Fujairah is a beautiful emirate; in stark contrast to Dubai, its craggy coastline, deserted beaches and dramatic wadis are barely touched by tourism.

Above: drummers near Dibba; windsurfer on the beach at Al Aqah.

DISTANCE 212km (132 miles) round trip

TIME A full day

START/END Dubai

POINTS TO NOTE

A rental car *(see p.108)* is required for this tour. Our route passes through the Sharjah suburbs and the mountain town of Masafi. At Masafi roundabout, turn left for Dibba and Al Aqah, not right on the more direct road to Fujairah town – we will make a clockwise loop towards Fujairah through Al Aqah and the Sharjah emirate port of Khor Fakkan.

After a while you might find that Dubai's beaches, for all their beauty, begin to feel slightly monotonous. The land is virtually flat and very little of the coastline retains the wildness of the desert interior. If sunbathing on a different kind of beach appeals, a day or overnight trip to the emirate of Fujairah to the east is highly recommended. The beaches on the UAE's eastern, Arabian Sea coast are wilder, more isolated, largely untouched by tourism than those on the west, and also have an impressive backdrop of mountains.

Arabian Sea
Fujairah, which has a coastline of 90km (56 miles), is the only emirate located entirely along the Gulf of Oman (Arabian Sea).

DESERT PARK

From Dubai, allow for a two-hour car journey to the coast of Al Aqah, north of Fujairah town. For the first part of the journey, take the E311 Emirates Road towards Sharjah International Airport, then follow the signs to Al Dhaid.

At Junction 8 of the Sharjah-Al Dhaid road you pass **Sharjah Natural History Museum and Desert Park ❶** (tel: 06 531 1999; www.shjmuseum. gov.ae; Sat, Mon–Wed 9am–7pm, Thur noon–7pm, Fri 2–10pm; charge). The park, set up in 1995, is a breeding ground for rare Arabian leopards, foxes, ibex, oryx and gazelles. At Al Dhaid, a small oasis town that is kept green by ancient *falaj* channels that run from the mountains, follow the signs to Masafi and Fujairah.

MASAFI

The scenery now starts to change from plains to mountains. In a small gorge about 5km (3 miles) before **Masafi ❷** you will pass through the **Friday Market**, which, despite its name, is open all week; here you can buy refreshments and souvenirs from stalls on either side of the highway. Local specialities

include inexpensive ornamental pots, many for holding candles, with patterns cut into the sides. You can also get good deals on machine-made carpets.

At Masafi, which produces a popular brand of UAE-bottled water, head left at the large roundabout, following signs for Dibba and Al Aqah. From here the road rises and falls through striking mountain scenery before passing south of Dibba town, which makes for a pleasant detour. If you are so inclined, follow the signs to the town centre.

DIBBA

Nestled below the Musandam Peninsula that divides the Arabian Gulf from the Arabian Sea and Indian Ocean, **Dibba** ❸ shares its coastline with Oman. In fact, the Dibba Bayah neighbourhood of Dibba is within Oman's territory – a strange arrangement whereby an enclave of Oman rather than the continuation of the UAE guards the Strait of Hormuz.

The remainder of the coastal town is administered by the emirates of Fujairah (Dibba Muhallab) and Sharjah (Dibba Al Hisn). Dibba Al Hisn's picturesque seafront, which is reminiscent of fishing villages on Oman's Batinah coast, offers a great view of the sweep of the bay and the mountains on either side. The *hisn*, or fort, from which it gets its name is just one block behind the corniche.

Arabian Peninsula

Continuing along the corniche with the Arabian Sea on your right, you

Above from far left: beach at Al Aqah; decorative pots for sale near Dibba.

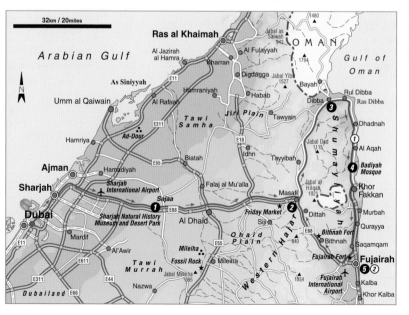

Snoopy Island

'Snoopy', the lovable beagle in the Peanuts comic strip by Charles Schulz, is recalled every time sunbathers at Fujairah's Sandy Beach Motel glance across at a rocky outcrop 100m (330ft) off shore. From a certain angle, 'Snoopy Island' resembles the comic strip pooch daydreaming atop his dog house.

Below: the oldest mosque in the UAE, at Badiyah.

will soon pass a sign marking the border with **Oman** (no paperwork required). After driving straight across at a small roundabout and then through an area with roadside flood markers, turn right onto a stony track and park. The beach is off to your right, but here, away from the sea, you may see thousands of fish lying in the sun: sardines that local fishermen have left to dry before they are processed into fertiliser.

Though isolated, this area has a rich history: in 633AD the Muslim forces of Caliph Abu Baker waged a great battle on this spot to suppress a local rebellion and claim the Arabian peninsula for Islam. Close to where your car is

parked you will see an enormous cemetery that contains some 10,000 stone markers on the graves of those who lost their lives in the battle.

Resort Hotels

Back in the car, retrace your route through Dibba, following the signs to Fujairah. The road south follows the coast here, with the Arabian Sea to your left and the mountains on your right. After the large, modern **Fujairah Rotana** (tel: 09 244 9888; www.rotana.com) and **Le Meridien Al Aqah** (tel: 09 244 9000; www.starwoodhotels.com) resort hotels – options for an overnight stay and food, *see* 🍴① – look out for signs indicating a left turn to the **Sandy**

Beach Motel (tel: 09 244 5555; www. sandybm.com). Here, for an entrance fee of Dhs50 per person, you can swim and snorkel off the private beach on Snoopy Island *(see margin, left)*, where the fish are colourful, and you may even encounter a reef shark.

FUJAIRAH

Continuing along the coast towards Fujairah city you quickly come to the historic 15th-century **Badiyah Mosque** ❹ (daily 24hrs; free) the oldest mosque in the UAE, on the right of the road. A brief stop here is highly rewarding, since non-Muslims are allowed to go inside the mosque, and there are stunning views of the coastal vegetation, sea and mountains from the watchtower above it.

Khor Fakkan, which is actually in the emirate of Sharjah thanks to another of the border anomalies in the region, is the next major town along the coast. Though it is not worth stopping here, the picturesque setting (seen on the UAE's Dhs5 note), the corniche and the container port can be viewed from the car as you pass through.

Fujairah ❺ itself is a pleasant city (good restaurants here include **Neptunia**, see ⓘ②), large enough to warrant its own airport, but there is not a great deal here to encourage visitors to linger, with the notable exception of the UAE's grandest fortress.

Fujairah Fort (tel: 09 222 9085; Sun–Thur 7.30am–6pm, Fri 2–6pm; charge), on the Masafi side of the city, was attacked by the British in colonial times and has parts dating back 500 years, making it the oldest fort in the UAE. Set against a stunning mountain backdrop, the fort forms the centrepiece of **Fujairah Heritage Village**, an ongoing restoration project that will see former palaces and homes opened to the public.

Bithnah Fort

Just before you complete our clockwise loop of Fujairah emirate at the large roundabout in Masafi, before heading back to Dubai via Al Dhaid and the Sharjah suburbs, look out for **Bithnah Fort** in the quiet village of Bithnah, to the right of the highway as it twists and turns through the mountains. Located in a mountain oasis setting, it is reminiscent of the great forts of northern Oman.

Above from far left: rope and fishing floats on Dibba beach; Fujairah Fort.

Bullfighting

Traditional Arab sports such as falconry and camel racing are not suited to the terrain of the east coast. As a result, the large Brahmin bull, which has worked for centuries in the area's palm groves, is bred to compete. The contest is between two large, pampered bulls, each weighing a tonne (ton) or more and fed on a diet of milk, honey and meal. The bulls try to force each other to the ground. Winners are also declared if an opposing bull turns and flees. The sport was possibly introduced in the 16th century by the Portuguese, although it may also pre-date Islam with its source in Persia, where the bull was once worshipped. The Fujairah contests are held on weekends in winter, near the palm groves off the Kalba/Oman road.

Food and Drink 🍴

① THE VIEWS

Le Meridien Al Aqah Beach Resort, Al Aqah; tel: 09 244 9000; lunch daily 12.30–3pm; $$–$$$
As the name suggests, this hotel venue on a rugged, fairly isolated stretch of coastline offers diners a fine view of the beach and the Arabian Sea. Good-value international buffet lunch served daily.

② NEPTUNIA

Hilton Fujairah Resort, Fujairah; tel: 09 222 2411; buffet daily noon–3pm; $$
Located in the city of Fujairah, the Hilton's Neptunia outlet offers a sea view with its excellent-value international lunch buffets. The hotel's nearby beach café offers an alternative à-la-carte menu.

ABU DHABI

Thought short on 'sights', the federal capital of the Emirates has plenty to offer visitors, from ancient archaeological sites and inspiring architecture to swanky hotels and fabulous beaches.

DISTANCE 238km (147 miles) round trip
TIME A full day
START/END Abu Dhabi
POINTS TO NOTE
Abu Dhabi is well served by buses from Dubai. The E1 service departs Al Ghubaiba Bus Station in Bur Dubai every 40 minutes between 6.20am and 9.40pm. The fare is Dhs15 one way. Taxis are a more expensive option (Dhs250 one way). For the greatest flexibility, opt for a rental car. The drive is straightforward and quick – follow the Abu Dhabi signs along Sheikh Zayed Road (E11). Allow 1½hrs either way.

Above: Al Maqta Bridge; tower of Al Hosn Palace.
Below: Emirates Palace Hotel.

In the past Abu Dhabi, the federal capital of the UAE, has had a rather cool approach to tourism, and tourists have been cool about it. With more than 94 per cent of the UAE's oil reserves (some 10 per cent of the world's total) under its sea and sands, it has not needed to diversify its economy and rely on tourism in the way that Dubai has. Consequently in the past, few visitors to Dubai considered it a worthwhile excursion.

However, oil-rich Abu Dhabi is slowly waking up to the benefits of world-renowned visitor-related projects, not the least of which is the international status they can confer upon a city. Accordingly, it has launched some of the most exciting projects in the UAE, emulating and at times eclipsing neighbouring Dubai.

Located on an island, Abu Dhabi is accessed via the Al Maqta Bridge, which is to be replaced by a design by Iraqi architect Zaha Hadid to its right. The old watchtower, which is visible from the bridge, can be seen in early black-and-white photographs of the city, when camel trains crossed from the mainland to the island at low tide.

Urban Regeneration

The formerly sleepy capital is currently in the throes of an exciting regenera-

tion period, notably with the addition of several new museums designed by internationally acclaimed architects. Although the big-name museums are still some years from opening, the projects have invigorated the capital, and the buzz is worth experiencing.

Due to be completed in 2012, the **Saadiyat Island Cultural District** will feature an unprecedented number of institutions by world-famous architects, including the Guggenheim Abu Dhabi contemporary art museum, by Canadian-born, American-based Frank Gehry (who also designed the iconic Guggenheim in Bilbao), the Louvre Abu Dhabi classical art museum (the first Louvre outside France), by French architect Jean Nouvel, a performing arts centre by Hadid and a maritime museum by Japanese architect Tadao Ando. Elsewhere in the city, British architect Norman Foster is working on the new Central Market.

On **Yas Island**, a Formula 1 racetrack has been designed by acclaimed F1 architect Hermann Tilke. The first F1 Grand Prix in the UAE will take place in Abu Dhabi in 2009, when Abu Dhabi joins nearby Bahrain on the international F1 calendar.

AL HOSN PALACE

The historic heart of the city is the **Al Hosn Palace ❶** or 'White Fort' (closed for renovation until 2009), Abu Dhabi's oldest building, located in the grounds of the Cultural Foundation on Khaled Bin Al Waleed Street, a couple

Above from far left:
Al Hosn Palace;
heading for the shops;
desert sunset; interior
of the Emirates
Palace Hotel.

'Father of the Gazelle'
Abu Dhabi means 'Father of the Gazelle'. According to local lore, the city was founded in 1793 after Bedu hunters from the Bani Yas tribe in the desert interior chased a gazelle to the coast. Chancing upon a freshwater spring, they saw the area was habitable and finally settled here.

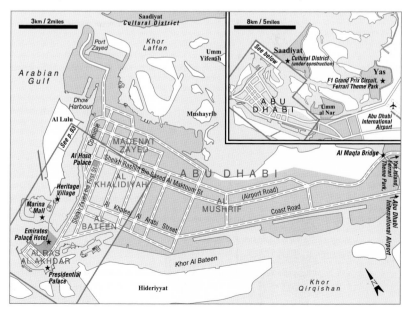

Sports Events

Abu Dhabi already has a world-class sporting event in the form of the European Tour-sanctioned Abu Dhabi Golf Championship, held at Abu Dhabi Golf Club in January. Among the big names to play here are Retief Goosen, Padraig Harrington, Sergio Garcia and Henrik Stenson. Previous champions include Chris DiMarco of the US and Paul Casey of England.

Ferrari Theme Park

Abu Dhabi is home to the world's first Ferrari Theme Park (open from 2008). Located on Yas Island, the venue for Abu Dhabi's Formula 1 Grand Prix from 2009, the theme park features family rides, a race track and driving school, virtual simulations and an exhibition on the history of the Italian carmaker. In 2007, Abu Dhabi was the starting point for Ferrari's 60th anniversary 50-nation world tour.

of blocks from the corniche at the top of the island. Built in 1793, the year the city was established, it was the residence of the ruling Al Nahyan family before finally becoming a visitor attraction. The original fort was built to protect the town's well, and the outer walls and tower were added at a later date. Today, its ancient battlements stand in stark contrast to the high-rise office, apartment and hotel buildings that surround it.

Food and Drink 🍴

① MAWAL

Hilton Abu Dhabi, Corniche Road West (1st Street); tel: 02 681 2773; daily 12.30–3.30pm and 7.30pm–2.30am; $$$$
This highly regarded, award-winning Lebanese restaurant offers mezze, grills and seafood. In the evenings it has live music and bellydancing.

② THE CAFÉ

Emirates Palace Hotel, Corniche West Street; tel: 02 690 7999; daily 6.30am–1am; $$$–$$$$
The opulent Emirates Palace Hotel, an Abu Dhabi landmark, is a fine setting for a memorable – if expensive – high tea, served in the lobby level café from 4–7pm daily, though the venue is open daily as above. Advance booking required.

③ HAVANA CAFÉ

Near Marina Mall, Breakwater; tel: 02 681 0044; daily 9am–2am; $$
The mainly Arabic menu includes international fare such as sandwiches and pizza. Excellent views across the Abu Dhabi waterfront to the high rises along the Corniche. Patio and rooftop seating available in the cooler months.

Situated opposite Al Hosn, at the junction of Sheikh Zayed the First and Al Maktoum, the **Abu Dhabi Cultural Foundation** ❷ (tel: 02 621 5300; Sat–Thur 8am–10pm, Fri 5–10pm; free) takes pride of place; it is the only arts centre of its kind in the region. This centre was set up under the patronage of Sheikh Zayed and runs a busy programme of artistic events, including the Emirates Film Festival and an international book fair.

THE CORNICHE

A short walk along Khaled Bin Al Waleed Street leads to the 8-km (5-mile) long corniche, the longest in the UAE and the backdrop for the annual Red Bull Air Race in April. The best time to visit is during the Friday weekend in winter, when the population of Abu Dhabi seems to head down here for picnics or an afternoon walk to enjoy the cool sea breeze. The several nearby parks are packed with kite-flyers on Fridays and public holidays. The corniche is home to **Mawal**, *see* 🍴①, in the Hilton Abu Dhabi.

Emirates Palace Hotel

To the west, the corniche continues towards the presidential palace and the landmark **Emirates Palace Hotel** ❸, *see* 🍴②, one of the most extraordinary, opulent, ultra-luxurious hotels in the world. This sprawling icon, constructed in traditional Arabian style, has 100 decorative domes. It is best viewed across the water from the promenade in front of the Marina Mall, but don't be afraid

to venture past the security gate for high tea in the hotel itself.

On the Breakwater near Marina Mall is the 1,600-sq-m (17,223-sq-ft) **Heritage Village** ❹ (tel: 02 681 4455; Mon–Thur and Sat 9am–1pm, 5–9pm, Fri 5–9pm; free), which illustrates the history of the emirate before oil revenues transformed the local landscape. There is an exhibition of Bedouin tents, a reconstruction of a palm house, old fishing villages and traditional souks. In addition, it offers a fabulous view of the Abu Dhabi skyline across the water. The **Havana Café**, *see* ⑪③, is near here.

ABU DHABI DHOWS

Located on the other side of the Emirates Palace Hotel from the Break- water, close to the InterContinental Hotel on the west of the island, is **Al Bateen Dhow Building Yard** ❺, one of the few surviving traditional boat-yards in the UAE. Visitors are very welcome to wander around, where piles of teak planks lie ready to be shaped into graceful wooden sailing dhows, the look of which has changed little over the centuries.

On the subject of dhows, if time allows, consider making a visit to Abu Dhabi's Dhow Harbour, on the north-east corner of the island, at the other end of the corniche from the Dhow Building Yard, near Port Zayed. From here you can take an evening cruise on a traditional wooden dhow and enjoy a fine Arabic dinner. A fitting way to end this tour.

Above from far left: local boy and horse; scaling a palm tree; romantic moment on the beach; along the Corniche.

Above: traditional hanging jar; water-front board game.

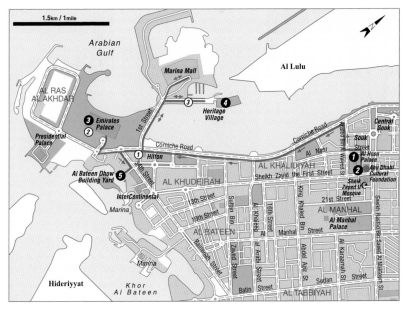

DIRECTORY

A user-friendly alphabetical listing of practical information, plus hand-picked hotels and restaurants, clearly organised by area, to suit all budgets and tastes.

A

AGE RESTRICTIONS

Car-rental agencies require drivers to be at least 21 or 22 years old. This rises to 25 and 30 depending on the vehicle category. Children under 10 are not allowed to sit in the front passenger seat of cars. Entry to bars and nightclubs varies between 18 (Waxy O'Conner's) and 21 (eg Irish Village and Trilogy). On the water, the minimum age for activities such as water skiing and parasailing is seven or eight, but it also depends on the weight of the child (minimum 40kg/88lb). For diving lessons, the minimum age for junior open water training is 10, but kids can begin learning in a pool from the age of eight.

ALCOHOL

Alcohol is only available in hotel and club restaurants and bars. Restaurants in malls and elsewhere outside the hotels are not permitted to serve alcoholic beverages. Never drink alcohol in public, as it is strictly illegal.

B

BUDGETING

Dubai is an expensive city to visit, and if you don't shop around for the best deal, or keep a tight reign on your daily expenditure at restaurants and shopping malls, you'll quickly discover that it is very good at parting you from your cash.

Accommodation: The cost for a standard double room ranges from around Dhs350 per night in a one-star city centre hotel (not recommended) to Dhs575–1,000 at a four-star hotel, and Dhs1,000–3,500 at a five-star hotel.

Eating and Drinking: It is possible to pick up a filling sandwich in a street-level Lebanese restaurant or a curry in a no-nonsense Indian or Pakistani outlet for as little as Dhs15. Main courses in most decent Western-style, non-hotel restaurants are between Dhs25–45. For fine dining, budget upwards of Dhs55 per person for mains. For a three-course dinner for two with wine at a five-star hotel venue, budget for upwards of Dhs600.

Cans of soft drinks start at Dhs1 in shops, but are heavily marked up in restaurants. Freshly made juices cost between Dhs6–15. Imported alcoholic drinks are generally more expensive than they would be in the West.

Transport: Package deals arranged from your home country are likely to be cheaper than separately arranged air travel and accommodation. The best prices are found in low season (July–Sept), but that's because it is the hottest time of the year in the UAE.

Generally taxis are cheaper than those in Western cities, but the taxi fare from the airport is higher than from elsewhere in the city. Buses are seldom used by visitors, but bus tickets offer the best value, costing between Dhs1–3, while a creek crossing on an *abra* (water taxi) is Dhs1.

C

CHILDREN

Childcare facilities are on a par with those in the West. Most malls have changing facilities in the women's public toilets; some also have supervised indoor play areas.

CLIMATE

Summers are very hot and humid. From May to September, daytime temperatures are rarely below 40°C (104°F) with humidity up to 90 per cent. From October to April the weather resembles that of an exceptionally good European summer, with temperatures hovering around 30°C (mid-80s°F) and little or no humidity.

Evenings can feel a little chilly around January/February, and jumpers may be required. Annual rainfall is minimal (an average of 42mm /1½in), but downpours occur from January to March – and when it rains, it pours. Inland, Hatta is a little cooler, particularly at night in winter.

CLOTHING

Comfortable loose cottons suit the climate best, with peak caps or sun hats for optimum protection during the heat of the day. In terms of culture, while the most daring swimwear is acceptable on the beach, around town visitors should be more modest and avoid wearing very short shorts and dresses and tight tops. Outside Dubai, more care should be taken to avoid showing too much bare skin: everyone's upper arms should be covered, and women are advised to wear long skirts or trousers. Winter evenings can be surprisingly cool, so pack a cardigan or jumper.

CRIME AND SAFETY

Dubai is a relatively safe city. Although petty theft is common, major crimes are rare and the level of personal security is high. Many women feel comfortable on their own in the evening. However, while you can let your guard down to some extent, it is best to avoid complacency; take the same precautions you would take anywhere else.

The US-led 'war on terror' has led to increased concerns for the safety of citizens of countries associated with military activity in the region. The UAE is no exception and vigilance against terrorism is recommended. However, there have been no incidents, the country is an ally of the US, and ordinary Emiratis are generally friendly to Westerners.

Dubai Police has a special Tourist Security Department, tel: 800 4438.

CUSTOMS

The duty-free allowances entering the UAE are as follows: 2,000 cigarettes, 400 cigars or 2kg (4lb) loose tobacco, and – for non-Muslims – four 'units' of alcohol, a unit being a bottle of wine, liqueur or spirits and one half case of beer (12 cans). There are no limits on perfume.

Above from far left: shadows of children on horseback; arid desert climate.

Bookstores
Recommended bookshops in Dubai include Jashanmal Bookstore and Borders in the Mall of the Emirates; BookPlus in Ibn Battuta Mall and Dubai Festival City; and Magrudy's, with stores in Deira City Center and Dubai Festival City.

D

DISABLED TRAVELLERS

Dubai Simply Accessible, a special guide for travellers with disabilities, is published by Dubai Department of Tourism and Commerce Marketing (DTCM) and is available at the tourist information counters in most malls. An online version can be viewed on the DTCM website www.dubaitourism.ae (click on 'Special Needs Tourism' on the home page). Among the subjects covered are facilities at Dubai International Airport; specialist taxi transportation (tel: Dubai Transport, 04 224 5331); access to hotels, heritage sites (including Dubai Museum), desert tours (tel: North Tours, 04 337 1219), cinemas, parks and malls; specialised equipment suppliers; and specialist medical facilities. Parking provision for people with disabilities is on a par with many Western cities. Most hotels have ramps allowing for wheelchair access. In modern malls there's usually an elevator alternative to an escalator. Most toilets in the UAE have enlarged cubicles for wheelchair access.

E

ELECTRICITY

Voltage in Dubai is 220/240 volts, 50 cycles AC. British-style three-pin sockets are common; if needed, adaptors can be bought from Carrefour hypermarkets at Deira City Centre and Mall of the Emirates.

EMBASSIES

Australia: BurJuman Centre, Trade Centre Road; tel: 04 508 7100; www.uae.embassy.gov.ae.
Canada: Bank Street Building, Bur Dubai; tel: 04 314 5555; www.dfait-maeci.gc.ca.
France: API World Tower, Sheikh Zayed Road; tel: 04 332 9040; www.ambafrance-eau.org.
Ireland: Riyadh, Kingdom of Saudi Arabia; tel: +966 1 488 2300; www.embassyofireland-riyadh.com.
New Zealand: Riyadh, Kingdom of Saudi Arabia; tel: +966 1 488 7988; www.mfat.govt.nz.
South Africa: New Sharaf Building, Bank Street, Bur Dubai; tel: 04 397 5222; www.southafrica.ae.
UK: Al Seef Road, Bur Dubai; tel: 04 309 4444; www.britishembassy.gov.uk.
US: 21st Floor, Dubai World Trade Centre, Sheikh Zayed Road; tel: 04 311 6000; http://dubai.usconsulate. gov.

EMERGENCIES

As in the UK, the emergency number to call for the police is 999, but ambulances are on 998 and the fire service on 997. Dubai Police Headquarters can be reached on 04 229 2222. For Dubai Police's Tourist Security Department, dial 800 4438.

ETIQUETTE

Dubai is one of the more liberal Gulf cities, and nationals are both familiar with and reasonably tolerant of those

What's On
For listings of events and happenings in Dubai up to 14 days in advance try www.timeoutdubai. com. For planning further ahead, try www.dubai-online. com/events or www. whatsonwhen.com.

from other cultures. Even so, any extra effort to respect Arab sensibilities is greatly appreciated.

Do not try and rush things, particularly with officialdom, which likes to take its time even over matters of apparent urgency – patience is a virtue; don't photograph men without first asking their permission and never photograph or even stare at local women; don't offer alcohol to Muslims; don't show the soles of your feet when sitting among locals; don't eat, drink or smoke in public areas during the holy month of Ramadan – the penalties are severe; and never drink and drive – you could end up in jail for a month.

Away from the beach, dress modestly; and if time permits, do graciously accept any hospitality that's offered – a refusal would be considered rude.

F

FESTIVALS

January–February: Dubai Shopping Festival (DSF), a month-long, city-wide festival with discounts at participating outlets. The festival also includes heritage and entertainment events, funfairs and pyrotechnic shows daily on the Creek. At night, bright lights transform the city into a giant theme park. In 2007, Cirque du Soleil's *Quidam* was the biggest show ever held in the Middle East. (www.my dsf.com).

March: The three-day Dubai International Jazz Festival is held at an open-air venue at Dubai Media City. It regularly attracts some of the best jazz performers in the world. (www. dubaijazzfest.com).

July–August: A summer version of DSF *(see above)*, the Dubai Summer Surprises (DSS) is another retail happening with most events tending to be held indoors, in malls. (www.my dsf.com).

November: The Dubai Airshow is a biennial extravaganza of a trade event that is closed to the public. From the streets around Dubai International Airport, however, you can see the afternoon flying displays by formation teams such as Britain's Red Arrows. The gala dinner is invitation-only, but the post-dinner concert by a big-name international star is open to the public. For more details, see www.dubaiair show.org.

December: National Day is a three-day holiday in the first week of December that marks the founding of the UAE in 1971. Parks and public places host cultural activities such as folk dancing, and at night the city is festooned in lights.

The Dubai International Film Festival (DIFF), which was inaugurated in 2004, attracts film-makers and stars from Hollywood, Bollywood and the Middle East. The red-carpet events and most screenings, which members of the public can buy tickets for, are held at Madinat Jumeirah. (www.dubaifilm fest.com).

FURTHER READING

Arabian Destiny by Edward Henderson, (Motivate, 1999). The memoirs of a long-term UAE resident and a gripping account of the country's evolution.

Rashid's Legacy by Graeme Wilson (Media Prima, 2006). A detailed history of the development of Dubai, with particular attention given to Sheikh Rashid and his sons.

From Trucial States to United Arab Emirates by Frauke Heard-Bey (Longmans, 1996) covers all aspects of life in the UAE.

G

GAY AND LESBIAN

Homosexuality is not tolerated in the UAE and is officially illegal, so discretion is strongly advised.

H

HEALTH

Hygiene/General Health: Dubai is a modern, reasonably clean city. Its public lavatories are well maintained (the WCs are mostly Western-style), and it is safe to drink the tap water, though most residents prefer to drink bottled water, which is advisable anyway outside of Dubai. One of the most popular brands of bottled water is the locally produced Masafi.

Due to widespread construction work, the air in Dubai is very dusty, so people who battle with asthma or their sinuses might suffer.

Medical/Dental Services: Healthcare is of a high standard in Dubai, but expensive, so it is wise to take out travel insurance. There are good government hospitals as well as numerous private clinics. The main emergency hospital is the government-run Rashid Hospital (tel: 04 337 4000) near Maktoum Bridge in Bur Dubai; emergency treatment is free here. A consultation with a doctor in non-emergency cases costs around Dhs100.

Alternatively, there is a government-affiliated Iranian Hospital (tel: 04 344 0250) on Al Wasl Road. Charges here are around Dhs50 per consultation.

For emergencies with children, Al Wasl Hospital (tel: 04 324 1111), across the highway from Wafi City, is a renowned paediatric hospital.

Dental problems can be dealt with by the American Dental Clinic (tel: 04 344 0668) or the Swedish Dental Clinic (tel: 04 223 1297).

Pharmacies: For details of 24-hour pharmacies, consult the listing in the local press or contact the Dubai Municipality's emergency number (tel: 04 221 5555 or 800900).

Vaccinations: No special inoculations are required prior to visiting the UAE.

HOURS AND HOLIDAYS

Business Hours: Government offices work from 7 or 7.30am–1.30pm Sun–

Thur. International companies keep the hours of 9am–5pm Sun–Thur. Local companies and shops typically open 8 or 9am–1/1.30pm and 4/4.30–8pm Sat–Thur. Generally, banks are open 8am–1pm Sat–Thur; closed Fri. Larger shopping malls open from 10am–10pm Sat–Thur and on Fri from around 2pm–late evening. A Fri–Sat weekend was introduced in 2006, where Friday equates to a Sunday in the West.

Public Holidays: Religious holidays are governed by the Islamic *(Hegira)* calendar and therefore do not fall on fixed dates. The main holidays are as follows: *Eid Al Fitr* (the end of Ramadan); *Eid Al Adha* (during the month of the *Haj*, or pilgrimage to Mecca); the ascension of the Prophet; the Prophet's birthday; and Islamic New Year. Check with the Ministry of Information and Culture: www.uae interact.com for dates. Other public holidays are New Year's Day (1 Jan) and National Day (2 Dec).

I

INSURANCE

Visitors should take out the standard policies that cover loss of property and emergency medical care.

INTERNET

Emirates Internet & Media (EIM), a subsidiary of the national telecommunications company Etisalat, is the main provider of Internet services in the UAE. Access to certain websites may be blocked. Internet connectivity is available in the guest rooms and business centres of larger hotels.

Elsewhere, Internet cafés can be found at various locations, including the Dune Centre, Satwa (tel: 04 345 3390; www.internetcafe.ae) and the F1 Net Cafe (tel: 04 345 1232; www. f1netcafe-dubai.com) in the Palm Strip Mall, Jumeira; the charges are Dhs12 per hour. There are also an increasing number of hot spots offering free wireless connectivity for laptop users. These include Coffee Bean & Tea Leaf on Jumeira Road, and French Connection café and Starbucks on Sheikh Zayed Road.

L

LANGUAGE

The official language is Arabic, but English is widely spoken and understood. It's unlikely that you'll encounter any difficulty using English in hotels, restaurants and shopping malls, but it could be useful to learn a few words and phrases in Arabic:

hello *marhaba*
welcome *ahlan wa-sahlan (ahlan)*
peace be with you (greeting)
as-salaam alaykum
and with you be peace (response)
wa-alaykum as-salaam
good morning *sabah al khayr*
good morning (response)
sabah al nour

Health Requirements
Do note that an immunisation certificate for cholera and yellow fever will be required if you are arriving from an infected area, such as parts of Africa and South America.

good evening *masaa al khayr*

good evening (response)*masaa al nour*

my name is... *ana ismi...*

what is your name? *shou ismac?*

how are you? *kayf haalak?*

well *zein*

you're welcome *afwan*

please *min fadlak*

thank you *shukran*

yes *naam*

no *la*

goodbye, peace be with you
maa as-salaama

LEFT LUGGAGE

The left luggage facility at Dubai International Airport is located in Arrivals (tel: 04 216 1734). At time of printing the cost for a normal size case was Dhs10 for 12 hours. Other options for left luggage are limited to the hotel you have been staying in, which should be willing to hold your luggage for a few hours after you have checked out.

LOST PROPERTY

There are many stories of lost property being returned. The key is to follow up with the relevant authority or organisation in the general area where your property may have been lost. This might include a local police station, mall management office, taxi company, hotel or bar. It's always worth putting a call in. The number for lost property (Baggage Services) at Dubai International Airport is 04 224 5383.

M

MEDIA

Newspapers: Local English-language newspapers are the broadsheet *Gulf News*, *Khaleej Times*, *The Gulf Today*, and the tabloid *Emirates Today* and *7 Days*. Foreign newspapers and English-language publications such as the *International Herald Tribune*, *USA Today* and *Weekly Telegraph* can be found in supermarkets. Most British newspapers arrive a day late, with the exception of *The Times* and *The Sunday Times*, which are also printed in Dubai. The main sources of information on events are *Time Out Dubai* and *What's On* listings magazines.

Radio: This is the best medium for getting a feel for Dubai's social scene. English-language talk radio made a welcome entry to the UAE in the form of Dubai Eye on 103.8 FM. Its programming covers current affairs, sport and general lifestyle matters, with panel discussions and phone-ins. Music stations broadcasting in English include Dubai 92 (92 FM), Channel 4 (104.8 FM), Emirates Radio 1 (99.3 FM and 100.5 FM) and Emirates Radio 2 (90.5 FM and 98.5 FM).

Television: Dubai's English-language TV station is the government-run Dubai One, which broadcasts Western movies and TV programmes, but has a local English-language news programme, Emirates News, at 8.30pm daily. Hotels also offer satellite and

cable television with international news channels such as CNN and Sky.

MONEY

Cash Machines: There are globally linked ATM points at banks, malls and some hotels.

Credit Cards: Major cards such as Visa, MasterCard, American Express and Diners Club are widely accepted in hotels, restaurants and shops. However, if you plan to bargain, it's better to have cash.

Currency: The UAE dirham (abbreviated to Dhs or AED). One dirham is 100 fils, and, at the time of printing (and since 1980), it was value-linked to the US dollar at Dhs3.67.

Money Changers: More convenient than banks in terms of opening hours and their location in busy shopping areas, money changers also offer better rates than banks. Among them are Al Ansari Exchange (tel: 04 397 7787), Al Fardan Exchange (tel: 04 228 0004), and Thomas Cook Al Rostamani (tel: 04 227 3690). All currencies accepted.

Taxes: A tax and service charge of between 15 and 20 per cent is added to hotel bills. Check that this is included in prices quoted.

Tipping: This is not compulsory, but most people do tip. Ten per cent should suffice, but you can give less in restaurants where a service charge has been added to the bill. Supermarket employees who pack and carry bags and petrol pump attendants who clean windscreens are also tipped, but in coins rather than notes.

Travellers' Cheques: Easily exchanged at hotels, banks and money changers, travellers' cheques are also sometimes accepted in major shops. Banks are generally open Sat–Thur 8am–1pm only. Money exchanges located in malls and souks keep shop hours.

P

PHOTOGRAPHY

Never take photographs of government buildings or military installations. Do not photograph people (especially women) without first asking permission.

POLICE

Dubai's police force has a low-key, but visible presence across the emirate: its green-and-white BMW and Mercedes patrol cars are a common sight on main highways and in residential neighbourhoods. During rush hour, the traffic flow at busy intersections is typically managed by police motorcyclists.

The emergency number for the police is 999. The toll-free number for general information, including details about the force's new Department for Tourist Security, is 800 4438. The police website is www.dubaipolice. gov.ae. (*See also Crime and Safety, p.97.*)

Maps
Dubai is changing so rapidly that maps of the city quickly become out of date. A good option is Dubai Municipality's Dubai Tourist Map, which is widely available in the city's hotel shops and book stores. GEOprojects produces a 1:750,000 scale map of the UAE with city maps of central Dubai and other key cities: www.geoprojects. net/uae.htm.

صندوق إيداع الرسائل

LETTER MAIL BOX

Population

Dubai's population is constantly on the rise; around 1.4 million people live in the city, with men outnumbering women by 3:1. Around 80 per cent of the total population are expatriates. Asian immigrants account for the bulk of these, and you may well hear as much Hindi, Urdu, Malayalam and Tagalog as Arabic, or possibly even more.

POST

Dubai's Central Post Office (Sat–Thur 8am–8pm; Fri 5–9pm) is located on Zabeel Road in Karama. There are smaller post offices around the city, including in Deira (near the Avari Hotel), Satwa (near Ravi's restaurant), Jumeira (on Al Wasl Road) and at the international airport.

The cost of sending an airmail letter to Western countries is around Dhs3–6 and a postcard around Dhs1–2. Allow 10 days for delivery. International courier companies operating in Dubai include DHL (tel: 800 4004), FedEx (tel: 800 4050) and UPS (tel: 800 4774).

R

RELIGION

Islam

Islam is the official religion of the UAE. Nationals are mostly Sunni Muslims.

Christianity

There is freedom of worship for Christians in church compounds on the understanding that they don't proselytise. Christian churches are grouped along Oud Metha Road in Bur Dubai and in Jebel Ali Village. They include Dubai Evangelical Church Centre (DECC, tel: 04 884 6630), the Anglican Holy Trinity (tel: 04 337 0247) and the Roman Catholic St Mary's (tel: 04 337 0087). The main services are held on Friday – the local weekend. Bibles for personal use can be carried into the country.

S

SMOKING

In general, the attitude to smoking is similar to that in Western nations. In 2005, the UAE ratified the World Health Organisation Framework Convention on Tobacco Control (WHO FCTC), under which it must adhere to international standards on tobacco-control measures, such as reducing exposure to passive smoking in public places. Anti-tobacco laws came into effect in two phases in May and September 2007. Now smoking in malls is only permitted in designated areas. During Ramadan, smoking in public anywhere is forbidden during daylight hours.

T

TELEPHONES

Direct international telephone dialling is available from all phones. Local calls within Dubai are free from a subscriber's phone. You should not have a problem finding coin- and card-operated public telephones on the streets and in shopping malls. Pre-paid phone cards, which cost Dhs30, are available from Etisalat, shops, supermarkets and service stations. Hotels tend to charge a premium for calls. Roaming mobile users will gain access to the local GSM service. As elsewhere, the code for dialling internationally from the UAE is 00 followed by the relevant national code and local number.

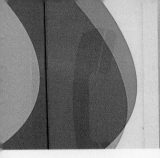

Local telecoms provider Etisalat can be contacted by dialling 101 or 144. The number for directory enquiries is 181. Assistance is provided in English as well as Arabic. Automated answering systems in Dubai tend to begin in Arabic, so hold on for instructions in English.

The international dialling code for the UAE is 971. Dubai's city code is 04 (omit the zero when dialling from overseas). The prefix for mobile numbers in the UAE is 050 or 055 (again, omit the zero when dialling from overseas). US access codes are as follows: AT&T 800121; MCI Worldcom 800111; Sprint 800131.

TIME DIFFERENCES

GMT (UCT) +4 hours, BST +3 hours.

TOILETS

Hotels and restaurants have Western-style toilets. In malls and other public places there's usually a combination of Western-style and squat toilets.

TOURIST INFORMATION

The Government of Dubai Department of Tourism and Commerce Marketing (DTCM; tel: 04 223 0000; www.dubaitourism.ae) is the emirate's official tourism promotion organisation. DTCM's information centres in Dubai include a kiosk at Dubai International Airport's arrivals hall, and desks in the following malls: Deira City Centre, BurJuman Centre, Wafi City,

Mercato and Ibn Battuta. There's also an office in Baniyas Square, Deira. The head office is on floors 10–12 of the National Bank of Dubai building on the Deira Creekside.

International Offices:

UK & Ireland: First Floor, 125 Pall Mall, London SW1Y 5EA; tel: +44 207 7839 0580; e-mail: dtcm_uk@ dubaitourism.ae.

North America: 25 West 45th Street, Suite #405, New York, NY 10036; tel: +1 212 719 5750; e-mail: dtcm_usa@ dubaitourism.ae.

Australia & New Zealand: Level 6, 75 Miller Street, North Sydney, NSW 2060; tel: +61 2 9956 6620; e-mail: dtcm_aus@dubaitourism.ae.

South Africa: PO Box 698, 1 Orchard Lane, Rivonia 2128, Johannesburg; tel: +27 11 785 4600; e-mail: dtcm_sa@ dubaitourism.ae.

TOURS

The leading tour companies offering desert safaris and 'wadi-bashing' trips along dry river beds are Arabian Adventures (tel: 04 303 4888; www.arabian-adventures.com); Desert Rangers (tel: 04 340 2408; www.desertrangers.com); Net Tours (tel: 04 266 8661; www. nettoursdubai.com); Orient Tours (tel: 04 282 8238; www.orienttours. ae); and Voyagers Xtreme (tel: 04 345 4504; www.turnertraveldubai.com).

For hot-air ballooning over the desert

contact Balloon Adventures Dubai (tel: 04 273 8585; www.ballooning.ae).

The Sheikh Mohammed Centre for Cultural Understanding (tel: 04 353 6666; *see pp.30 and 70*) organises visits to the homes of local Emirati families. The centre also runs hour-long English-language tours of Jumeira Mosque on Sundays and Thursdays, beginning at 10am.

For details of helicopter and dhow tour operators, see the Walks and Tours section of this guide, *pp.62 and 64*.

TRANSPORT

Airports and Arrival

The main gateway is Dubai International Airport (tel: 04 224 5555; www.dubaiairport.com), which is 10 minutes away from central Deira and a 30- to 45-minute drive from the hotels on the Jumeira coast. Having undergone a US$4 billion expansion programme between the late 1990s and 2007, this bustling Middle East passenger and cargo hub has futuristic new terminals, a landmark air-traffic-control tower, and a large Dubai Duty Free area.

Home of the award-winning national carrier Emirates (www.emirates.com), Dubai airport is served by the major airlines and global alliance partners of Europe and Asia – British Airways, Virgin Atlantic, Lufthansa, KLM, Air France, Delta, Air India, Singapore Airlines, Malaysia and Thai among them. Direct flights from the US are provided by Emirates and Delta. The flight time to Dubai from Europe is around seven hours; 13 hours from New York.

The airport is busiest throughout the night. To speed you past the long queues at passport control when you arrive, consider booking the Marhaba ('Welcome') greeting service at least 24 hours in advance (tel: 04 224 5780, www.marhabaservices.com). The fee is Dhs80 per passenger from immigration. Note that the walk between the terminal and passport control is long: electric carts are provided for the elderly and travellers with disabilities.

Kiosks for tourist information, hotels, car-rental agencies and money exchanges are beyond the baggage reclaim area. Dubai Transport taxis are off to the left as you exit the airport building.

There is no airport departure tax on leaving Dubai.

Transport Within Dubai

Dubai Metro: The Dubai Metro light rail project is being phased in and should do much to alleviate the pressure on the city's increasingly traffic-logged streets. The 70-km (44-mile) network will have three routes – Red, Green and Purple – connecting Dubai International Airport with Deira, Bur Dubai and Jebel Ali. The elevated section of the Red line is a distinctive feature of Sheikh Zayed Road and will have stations at landmarks such as Emirates Towers and Burj Dubai. For more information, visit the Dubai Metro page on the website of Dubai's Roads and Transport Authority (RTA): www.rta.gov.ae.

Taxis: This is the best way to get around the city. Cabs are metered, air-

conditioned, and, mostly, clean and reliable. Taxis from the airport start with the meter at Dhs20, though in the city, the meter starts at around Dhs3. The fare from the airport to destinations in Deira and Bur Dubai will be around Dhs30–40, but will be considerably more (upwards of Dhs80) to the more distant resort hotels along the Jumeira coast. The main operators are Dubai Transport Corporation or DTC (tel: 04 208 0808), Cars Taxi (tel: 04 269 2900), Metro Taxi (tel: 04 267 3222) and National Taxi (tel: 04 339 0002).

In addition to the ivory-coloured metered taxis, there are also non-metered taxis. The fares of these should be negotiated before the journey is undertaken, starting at a minimum fare of around Dhs5 for short local journeys, and Dhs10–15 if you cross the Creek from one side of the city to the other.

Bus: Used mainly by lower-income workers, Dubai's bus service – which operates in Deira from Al Sabkha Bus Station between the Gold Souk and Beniyas Square, and in Bur Dubai from Al Ghubaiba Street – has undergone vast improvements in recent years but it's not really a convenient alternative to taxis for trips within the city. However, for longer journeys a bus can offer both a money-saving alternative to rental cars and an experience to remember. The bus for Hatta is the no. 16, which departs from the Gold Souk. The bus for Abu Dhabi is E1, which leaves from Bur Dubai bus station, near the HSBC building on the Creek. For information call 800 9090.

Water Taxi: The best way to appreciate the Creek and sample the bustle of daily life in the heart of the old city is to take

Left: a great way of getting around.

a water taxi, or *abra*. Fares are just Dhs1 for trips from Bur Dubai to Deira and vice versa, but for Dhs100 an *abra* captain would take you on a one-hour tour.

Water Bus: Introduced in 2007, the air-conditioned Water Bus operates commuter and tourist services from the various Creekside water taxi stations in Deira and Bur Dubai. Journeys on the dedicated tourist route, which operates between 8am and midnight, cost around Dhs25 per person.

Car: For a city that didn't have a single stretch of tarmac when oil was discovered, Dubai has an excellent road infrastructure. All the major car-rental agencies have offices here. To get a temporary driving licence, hand over your passport, national or international driving licence and two photographs and the agency will arrange the paperwork. International hire companies include Avis (tel: 04 295 7121), Budget (tel: 04 295 6667), Hertz (tel: 04 282 4422) and Thrifty (tel: 04 224 5404).

Remember to drive on the right, always carry your licence with you and never drink and drive – Dubai has a zero-tolerance policy on drink driving and the penalty for ignoring it is a month in jail. The wearing of seat belts is compulsory for drivers and front-seat passengers, and children under 10 aren't allowed to sit in the front passenger seat.

Speed limits are normally between 60kph (37mph) and 120kph (74mph). Lane discipline is bad, and reckless driving fairly common, so drive with caution at all times. On road signs, distances are indicated in kilometres.

If you're involved in a road accident, stop and wait for the police. A police report on every level of accident is required for insurance claims.

V

VISAS AND PASSPORTS

Visas are available on arrival at Dubai International Airport for business and

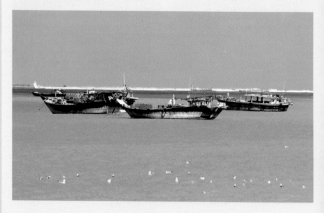

Right: idyllic shot of dhows out on the Creek.

Above from far left: couple admiring the view; receptionist at a desert resort.

leisure travellers from 33 countries, including the UK, Ireland, the US, Canada, Australia, and New Zealand. The visa (free to UK citizens) is valid for 60 days and can be renewed for a further 30 days at the Department of Immigration and Naturalisation (tel: 04 398 1010), near Trade Centre Roundabout, for around Dhs500.

Those who don't qualify for a visa on arrival, including South African citizens, can get a 30-day, non-renewable tourist visa through a hotel or tour operator sponsor. This should be arranged before entry to the UAE: visitors should ensure they have a fax copy of the visa with them and they should stop to collect the original at a designated desk in the airport before they head for passport control. The total cost is Dhs120.

WEBSITES

The following websites are useful sources of information:

- **7Days** www.7days.ae
- **AMEInfo** www.ameinfo.com
- **Dubai Duty Free** www.dubaidutyfree.com
- **Dubai International Airport** www.dubaiairport.com
- **Dubai Municipality** www.dm.gov.ae
- **Dubai Roads and Transport Authority (RTA)** www.rta.gov.ae
- **Emirates** www.emirates.com
- **Emirates Today** www.emiratestodayonline.com
- **Government of Dubai Department of Tourism and Commerce Marketing (DTCM)** www.dubaitourism.ae
- **Gulf News** www.gulfnews.com
- **Sheikh Mohammed Bin Rashid Al Maktoum** www.sheikhmohammed.co.ae
- **UAE Ministry of Information and Culture** www.uaeinteract.com
- **TimeOut Dubai** www.timeoutdubai.com

WEIGHTS AND MEASURES

The metric system is used in Dubai.

WOMEN

Unlike in neighbouring Saudi Arabia, in the UAE women are not expected to cover up in public (except when visiting Jumeira Mosque), and they are allowed to drive. One of the very few restrictions is at Dubai Youth Hostel (tel: 04 298 8151), part of the UAE Youth Hostel Association (www.uaeyha.com), where women travelling alone may be refused a booking. However, Dubai is generally one of the easiest places in the Middle East for lone women to travel around, and many feel comfortable on their own in the evening.

In terms of personal security, women are generally safe, but reports of rapes have been carried in the local press; exercise standard precautions and on no account accept lifts from men met in bars and nightclubs. Away from beaches and swimming pools, women are expected to dress modestly, as are men.

Coastal Hotels

Burj Al Arab

PO Box 74147, Jumeira Road,
Umm Suqeim; tel: 04 301 7777;
www.burj-al-arab.com; $$$$

The tallest all-suites hotel in the world, set on its own island off the Jumeirah Beach Hotel, the now iconic, sail-shaped Burj Al Arab offers the utmost in luxury accommodation. One night in a 225-sq-m (2,422-sq-ft) 'Panoramic' suite complete with butler service and a winding staircase to bed costs US$1,500. Each duplex has a laptop computer, 114-cm (45-in) television, Italian marble, Irish linen and ceiling mirrors in the bedrooms. Guests are ferried around in a fleet of white Rolls-Royces.

Dubai Marine Beach Resort & Spa

Jumeira Road, Jumeira 1, tel: 04 346 1111; www.dxbmarine.com; $$$

Not to be confused with Dubai Marina along the coast, Dubai Marine is the closest Jumeira beach resort to the city, a short walk across Jumeira Road from Jumeira Mosque. It offers 195 rooms in villa-style, low-rise buildings in a landscaped compound fronting on to a small beach. It also has some of the city's best nightspots, including Sho Cho's and Boudoir.

Grosvenor House

Dubai Marina, tel: 04 399 8888; www.grosvenorhouse.lemeridien.com; $$$

Although the 45-storey Le Meridien property is not located on the beach, it offers stunning views of the coast, and guests can use the beach facilities at the nearby Royal Meridien Beach Resort. Notable nightspots at the hotel include Bar 44 and Buddha Bar.

Jumeirah Beach Hotel

PO Box 11416, Jumeira Road,
Umm Suqeim; tel: 04 348 0000;
www.jumeirah.com; $$$

Designed to look like a wave to complement neighbouring Burj Al Arab's 'sail', the 26-storey Jumeirah Beach has 600 sea-facing rooms, a breathtaking atrium and a plethora of restaurants and bars.

Mina A'Salam

PO Box 75157, Madinat Jumeirah,
Umm Suqeim; tel: 04 366 8888;
www.jumeirah.com; $$$

The better value of two grand Arabian-themed hotels located within the fabulous Madinat Jumeirah Resort near Burj Al Arab (the other being Al Qasr). Mina A'Salam ('Port of Peace') is an Arabian-Nights fantasy linked to Souk Madinat Jumeirah by canals and paths.

The price indicator after each listing is based on two people sharing a standard double room for one night in high season (Nov–April) with tax and service charges included.

$$$$	More than US$1,000
$$$	US$500–1,000
$$	US$250–500
$	Less than US$250

Oasis Beach Hotel

PO Box 26500, off Al Sufouh Road, near Dubai Marina; tel: 04 399 4444; www.jebelali-international.com; $$

The best-value hotel on the coast and a good choice for families. The Oasis Beach has a pleasant beachfront with large terrace, pool bar, lawns and private beach, as well as the high level of service expected of a sister to the Jebel Ali and Hatta Fort hotels. The Oasis Beach Tower across the road offers a cost saving for groups sharing three- or four-bedroom apartments.

One & Only Royal Mirage

PO Box 37252, Al Sufouh Road; tel: 04 399 9999; www.oneandonly royalmirage.com; $$$

Located opposite Dubai Media City and one of Dubai's best hotels, this 250-room resort has fabulous decor, lush oasis greenery, superb restaurants and a fashionable nightspot: Kasbar. Resembling a traditional Arabic fortress, the hotel doubled as the sheikh's Marbella palace in the movie *Syriana*. A good choice for romantics.

The Ritz-Carlton Dubai

Al Sufouh Road/Dubai Marina, tel: 04 399 4000; www.ritzcarlton.com; $$$

A little bit of Andalusia in the Gulf, the low-lying, hacienda-style Ritz-Carlton has 138 rooms, all of which are sea-facing. More than any other hotel on the coast, it's a quiet retreat for rest and relaxation, far removed from the distractions and crowds of larger beach resorts. Its restaurants

include the highly rated La Baie (French) and Splendido (Italian).

City Hotels – South of the Creek

Dusit Dubai

Sheikh Zayed Road, tel: 04 343 3333; www.dusit.com; $$$

The Thai-owned Dusit is one of Sheikh Zayed Road's architectural wonders – the design of the building represents two hands pressed together in the traditional Thai greeting. Set on the Emirates Towers side of the highway near Interchange No. 1, the Dusit has 174 rooms, including suites and furnished apartments. Not surprisingly, its restaurants include the Thai Benjarong, though it has to be said, it is not the city's best.

Fairmont Dubai

PO Box 97555, Sheikh Zayed Road; tel: 04 332 5555; www.fairmont.com; $$$

Located at the Satwa end of Sheikh Zayed Road, the Fairmont is a good base for the Dubai International Exhibition Centre, and for exploring the city south of the creek, particularly if you're renting a car, as Jumeira and Nad Al Sheba are short drives away. The space-age interior boasts the popular Spectrum On One restaurant *(see p.121)* and a couple of hip nightspots.

Four Points Sheraton Bur Dubai

Khalid Bin Al Waleed Street (Bank Street); tel: 04 397 7444; www.four points.com/burdubai; $$$

Above from far left: pool at the Burj Al Arab; a relaxing corner at the Jumeirah Beach Hotel.

Finding a Deal
Dubai's hotels are not cheap, and the best deals are likely to be found through tour operators in your country of origin during the northern hemisphere summer. If you call hotels direct, most quoted room rates will not include 20 per cent tax and service charge or breakfast.

Dubai Districts
The majority of less expensive hotels can be found in Bur Dubai and Deira, while the most desirable five- to seven-star properties (with a few notable exceptions) are on Sheikh Zayed Road and the Arabian Gulf coast. Stretching from Jumeira through Umm Suqeim to Al Sufouh and Al Mina Al Siyahi, the coast is commonly referred to as 'Jumeira'. It may seem some distance on maps, but the hotels in this area are actually only 30 minutes' drive from the airport.

The four-star, 125-room Four Points Sheraton is set in the heart of downtown Bur Dubai. It makes an ideal base for exploring for the Creek and heritage sights such as Bastakiya, Al Fahidi Fort (Dubai Museum) and Bur Dubai Souk.

Golden Sands

PO Box 9168, Al Mankhool Street, Bur Dubai; tel: 04 355 5553; www.goldensandsdubai.com; $$

Comprising 11 separate deluxe apartment buildings rather than a star-rated hotel, Golden Sands offers self-catering options in the heart of the city that are popular with large families or groups that visit Dubai for events such as the Shopping Festival and Rugby Sevens. The more people sharing, the cheaper the cost, though for singles, couples and small families, the facilities don't justify the four-star pricing.

Grand Hyatt

PO Box 7978, Umm Hurair; tel: 04 317 1234; www.dubai.grand.hyatt.com; $$$

The 674-room Grand Hyatt dominates the highway on the Bur Dubai side of

---

The price indicator after each listing is based on two people sharing a standard double room for one night in high season (Nov–April) with tax and service charges included.

$$$$	More than US$1,000
$$$	US$500–1,000
$$	US$250–500
$	Less than US$250

Garhoud Bridge near Wafi City. The hotel is centrally located between the airport, Deira and Sheikh Zayed Road, has several quality restaurants, rooms with stunning city views and the 'super-club' MIX to boot.

Ibis World Trade Centre

PO Box 9544, Sheikh Zayed Road/ Trade Centre 2; tel: 04 332 4444; www.ibishotel.com; $

The stylish, comfortable, four-star Ibis is one of the city's best-value offerings, but given its location next to Dubai International Exhibition Centre, competition for its 210 rooms is intense during the October–May conference season.

Jumeirah Emirates Towers Hotel

PO Box 72127, Sheikh Zayed Road; tel: 04 330 0000; www.jumeirah.com; $$$

One of the tallest hotels in the world, the landmark Jumeirah Emirates Towers is in one of the two silver towers near the Dubai International Financial Centre (DIFC) and Dubai International Exhibition Centre. Hotel venues include Vu's restaurant and bar, but the nearby Boulevard has the Agency wine bar, Al Nafoorah Lebanese eatery and more besides.

Ramada

PO Box 7979, Al Mankhool Road, Bur Dubai; tel: 04 351 9999; www.ramadadubai.com; $$

The venerable Ramada is convenient for the Creek, the Bastakiya heritage

district, Dubai Museum, Dubai Old Souk and the BurJuman Centre shopping mall. It's also within walking distance of the many computer and electronics shops in the area.

Seashell Inn Hotel

Khalid Bin Al Waleed Street (Bank Street); tel: 04 393 4777; www.landmarkhotelsdubai.com; $$
This three-star, 98-room city centre hotel in the heart of downtown Bur Dubai is within walking distance of the heritage areas of Shindagha, Bur Dubai Souk, Al Fahidi Fort (Dubai Museum) and Bastakiya.

Shangri-La

PO Box 75880, Sheikh Zayed Road; tel: 04 343 8888; www.shangri-la.com; $$$
A 43-storey, Gotham-esque structure near Interchange No. 1, the Shangri-La has 301 guest rooms and suites, many with outstanding views of the Jumeira coast. Scenes from George Clooney's movie *Syriana* were shot in the hotel.

Towers Rotana

PO Box 30430, Sheikh Zayed Road; tel: 04 343 8000; www.rotana.com; $$
A smart business hotel on the Satwa/ Jumeira side of Sheikh Zayed Road with great evening venues such as Long's Bar and the Teatro restaurant.

XVA Gallery

PO Box 37304, Al Bastakiya; tel: 04 353 5383; www.xvagallery.com; $
No other paid accommodation in Dubai can compete with the XVA Gallery's authentic Arabian offering. More a guesthouse than a hotel – too small to qualify for a star-rating – the XVA is first and foremost an art gallery and coffee shop set around the inner courtyard of a restored home in the historic Bastakiya district *(see p.30)*. Its

eight guest rooms, furnished in the Arabian-style, are on the first-floor rooftop, which offers wonderful views of the Creek skyline, in particular the wind-towers on nearby buildings. A delightful, inspirational haven for artists and writers in particular.

City Hotels – North of the Creek

Al Bustan Rotana

PO Box 30880, Garhoud; tel: 04 282 0000; www.rotana.com; $$$

The large, light foyer immediately sets the tone. Classy and spacious, the Al Bustan is very convenient for the airport and Dubai Tennis Stadium, which has a number of restaurants to visit when you've tried the excellent venues in the hotel itself. Downtown Deira is a short cab-ride away.

Hilton Dubai Creek

PO Box 33398, Deira; tel: 04 227 1111; www.hilton.com; $$

This stylish, modern business hotel was designed by architect Carlos Ott and boasts Gordon Ramsay's Verre restaurant *(see p.118)*. The name might suggest a quayside setting, but the hotel is separated from the Creek by several lanes of traffic.

Radisson SAS Deira Dubai Creek

PO Box 476, Baniyas Road, Deira; tel: 04 222 7171; www.deiracreek. dubai.radissonsas.com; $$$

Possibly the best city-centre hotel with views of Dubai Creek, the Radisson is an excellent base from which to explore the souks of Deira. Formerly the Inter-Continental, this was the first five-star hotel in Dubai when it opened in 1975.

Hyatt Regency Dubai

PO Box 5588, Corniche Street, Deira; tel: 04 209 1234; www.dubai. regency.hyatt.com; $$

An imposing monolith dominating the mouth of Dubai Creek, the Hyatt Regency has excellent restaurants, including the Mediterranean Focaccia *(see p.32)*, and one of the few ice rinks in Dubai. The closest high-quality hotel to Dubai's Gold Souk.

Park Hyatt

Dubai Creek Golf & Yacht Club; tel: 04 602 1234; www.dubai.park. hyatt.com; $$$

The first Park Hyatt in the Middle East when it opened in 2005, this hotel is positioned as a 'city-centre luxury retreat'. It is a credible claim given its private Creekside setting next to Dubai Creek Golf & Yacht Club, and Deira City Centre and the Aviation Club tennis and restaurant complex are just nearby.

> The price indicator after each listing is based on two people sharing a standard double room for one night in high season (Nov–April) with tax and service charges included.
>
> $$$$ More than US$1,000
> $$$ US$500–1,000
> $$ US$250–500
> $ Less than US$250

UAE Youth Hostel Association

39 Al Nahda Road; tel: 04 298 8161; www.uaeyha.com; $

Located near Al Mulla Plaza, north of the airport, this is good, clean accommodation for men, women and families, although single women may be refused a booking if the hostel is busy with men. By international standards, the hostel is expensive, but relative to the Dubai market, the rooms here – singles, doubles and dorms – are an absolute bargain. The standards in this well-managed hostel can be likened to that in some three-star hotels.

Al Maha Resort

PO Box 7631, Dubai-Al Ain Road (E66); tel: 04 832 9900; www. al-maha.com; $$$$

Meaning 'gazelle' in Arabic, Al Maha offers the most Arabian accommodation in Dubai without any compromise on luxury. Not so much a hotel as a Bedu desert encampment of 30 luxury chalet 'tents' within a large nature reserve, this is Dubai's first eco-tourism resort. Activities include camel riding, falconry displays and desert safaris.

Bab Al Shams Desert Resort & Spa

PO Box 8168, Endurance City; tel: 04 832 6699; www.jumeirahbabal shams.com; $$

Located in the desert near the Endurance City horse-riding venue some 37km (23 miles) from Arabian Ranches, the Jumeirah group's Bab Al Shams ('Gate of the Sun') is popular with city residents as a weekend get-away and is a good alternative to the Al Maha Resort for the budget conscious.

Hatta Fort Hotel

PO Box 9277, Hatta; tel: 04 852 3211; www.jebelali-international.com; $$

Around an hour's drive from Dubai and set in 32ha (80 acres) of grounds in the Hajar Mountains near historic Hatta and the UAE border with Oman, the 50-room Hatta Fort is a popular weekend retreat. It makes a great base for wadi and desert adventures and the hotel also offers archery and shooting. Good value for money.

Above from far left: Park Hyatt; Al Bustan Rotana.

Camping
The UAE doesn't have any official campsites, but that doesn't stop local and expat residents camping in the desert dunes on weekends and national holidays. But the best and safest way for visitors to overnight in the desert is with a specialist tour company. Camping on Dubai's public beaches is not allowed without a permit from Dubai Municipality (tel: 04 221 5555).

Left: XVA Gallery.

Al Dahleez

Al Boom Tourist Village, Umm Hurair;
tel: 04 324 3000; daily noon–4pm
and 7pm–midnight; $$

This Creekside Arabic buffet restaurant near Garhoud Bridge offers good Emirati food and is popular with local families – a sure sign of authenticity. No alcohol. Dress: smart casual.

Bastakiah Nights

Bastakiya, Bur Dubai; tel: 04 353
7772; daily 12.30–11.30pm; $$$

This ambient Iranian-owned restaurant is located in an historic courtyard house near the Creek. The menu includes mezze and other Arabic dishes. No alcohol. Dress: smart casual.

Bateaux Dubai

Al Seef Road; tel: 04 399 4994;
boarding for the dinner cruise at
8pm daily; $$$$$

Floating restaurant offering an international menu and great Creek views.

Khazana

Al Nasr Leisureland, Umm Hurair;
tel: 04 336 0061; daily 12.30–
2.30pm and 7–11.30pm; $$$

Owned by Indian celebrity chef Sanjeev Kapoor, Khazana does excellent North Indian specialities in a village-style conservatory setting. Alcohol. Dress: smart casual.

Ravi's

Satwa Roundabout, Satwa; tel:
04 331 5353; Sat–Thu 5am–3am,
Fri 1.30pm–3am; $

Ravi's is to Pakistani cuisine what Automatic *(see p.119)* is to its Arabic equivalent. This extremely popular, no-frills curry house is located in a thriving neighbourhood and has outside seating on the street. No alcohol. Dress: casual.

Al Dawaar

Hyatt Regency Hotel, Deira; tel:
04 209 1234; www.dubai.regency.
hyatt.com; daily noon–3.30pm
and 7pm–11.30pm; $$$–$$$$

Dubai's only revolving restaurant is on the 25th floor and has amazing views north towards Sharjah and, in the opposite direction, to the Creek mouth, Shindagha and Port Rashid. An international buffet complements the visual feast. Alcohol. Dress: smart casual.

Al Mansour

Radisson SAS; tel: 04 222 7171;
boarding from the Deira Creekside
near the Radisson SAS at 8pm daily;
$$$$

Traditional dhow that plies the Creek for dinner cruise. Diners feast on a buffet with both Arabic and international food.

Price guide for a two-course meal for two, with a glass of wine each where alcohol is available:	
$$$$$	over Dhs500
$$$$	Dhs400–500
$$$	Dhs200–400
$$	Dhs100–200
$	below Dhs100

Benihana

Al Bustan Rotana Hotel, Garhoud;
tel: 04 282 0000; www.benihana.com;
daily noon–3pm and 7pm–midnight;
$$$

This teppanyaki and sushi restaurant with minimalist decor is a good choice on any evening, and on Tuesdays and Saturdays it offers all-you-can-eat sushi and sashimi promotions. Alcohol. Dress: smart casual.

Blue Elephant

Al Bustan Rotana Hotel, Garhoud; tel:
04 282 0000; www.blueelephant.com;
daily noon–3pm and 7–11.30pm; $$$

At this candidate for best Thai restaurant in Dubai, the wonderful food can be enjoyed in a Thai-village environment that complements the authentic cuisine. Alcohol. Dress: smart casual.

Café Chic

Le Meridien Dubai, Garhoud;
tel: 04 282 4040; daily 12.30–
2.45pm and 8–11.45pm; $$$$$

The elegant, stylish Café Chic is spread over two levels and serves authentic French food. The desserts, including hot chocolate soufflé, are particularly good. Alcohol. Dress: smart casual.

Da Vinci's

Millennium Airport Hotel, Garhoud;
tel: 04 282 3464; daily noon–
midnight; $$$

This Italian eatery is a Dubai institution. It offers the usual Italian staples,

Above from far left: chandelier at Al Nafoorah (see p.119); Almaz by Momo (see p.119).

Left: perfect presentation.

Children
If you are travelling with children, there are activity centres near the food courts at Deira City Centre, Mercato Mall and Mall of the Emirates. Many hotels offer all-you-can-eat brunch specials on Fridays.

represents good value for money and is run by friendly, efficient staff. Alcohol. Dress: smart casual.

JW's Steakhouse

JW Marriott Hotel, Deira; tel: 04 262 4444; daily 12.30–3.30pm and 7.30–11pm; $$$$$

JW's wonderful cuts are prepared with an American slant and flame-grilled to your taste. The decor is clubby, with panelled wood and deep leather chairs. Good wine list. Dress: smart.

Kiku

Le Meridien Dubai, Airport Road, Deira; tel: 04 282 4040; daily 12.30–3pm and 7–11pm; $$$

Kiku's enduring popularity among visiting Japanese businessmen confirms its reputation as one of the best Japanese restaurants in the city. Alcohol. Dress: smart casual.

Mazaj

Century Village, The Aviation Club, Garhoud; tel: 04 282 9952; daily noon–1am; $$$

Popular Lebanese place located along with a number of other restaurants in a lively, leafy plaza. Great alfresco dining. The club setting means that alcohol is served. Shisha also available. Dress: smart casual.

More

Behind Lifco Supermarket, near Welcare Hospital, Garhoud, tel: 04 283 0224; daily 8am–11pm; $$

A funky Dutch-owned bistro that is popular with media types who work nearby and Emirates cabin crew who live in the surrounding buildings. The international menu offers an amazing choice. A difficult place to beat for its combination of excellent atmosphere, quality, value and service.

Sukhothai

Le Meridien Dubai, Airport Road, Deira; tel: 04 282 4040; daily 2.30–3.30pm and 7.30pm–2.30am; $$$$

Consistently rated as one of the best Thai restaurants in Dubai, Sukhothai offers sumptuous dishes in an atmospheric wood-panelled interior. Alcohol. Dress: smart casual.

Verre

Hilton Creek, Deira; tel: 04 227 1111 www.hiltondubaiCreek.com; daily 7–11pm; $$$$$

The first overseas venture for UK celebrity chef Gordon Ramsay, Verre is highly recommended if you want to splash out. The minimalist decor ensures the focus is well and truly on the food. Alcohol. Dress: smart casual.

Sheikh Zayed Road and Jumeira

Al Mahara

Burj Al Arab, Jumeira Road; tel: 04 301 7600; www.burj-al-arab.com; daily 12.30–3pm and 7pm–12.30am; $$$$$

This seafood venue is reportedly Dubai's most expensive restaurant and certainly one of the city's plushest. Its centrepiece is the mother of all fish tanks. Alcohol. Dress: smart.

Almaz by Momo

Harvey Nichols, Mall of the Emirates, Sheikh Zayed Road; tel: 04 409 8877; Sat–Thur 10am–midnight, Fri 10am–1.30am; $$$

This is the Dubai version of the celebrity hang-out in London, established by Mourad 'Momo' Mazouz. Almaz offers mezze and traditional Moroccan mains in a trendy, contemporary North African-themed interior. Does not feel like it's attached to a mall. No alcohol. Dress: smart casual.

Al Nafoorah

Emirates Towers, Sheikh Zayed Road; tel: 04 319 8088; www.emirates towershotel.com/dining; daily 12.30–3pm and 8pm–12.30am; $$$

The best Lebanese restaurant in town, with a great-value lunch menu and pleasant terrace. Look out for Sheikh Mohammed, who drops in from time to time. Alcohol. Dress: smart casual.

Al Qasr

Dubai Marine Beach Resort & Spa, Jumeira Road; tel: 04 346 1111; Fri–Wed 12.30–3.30pm and 7.30pm–2am, Thur 12.30–3.30pm and 7.30pm–3am; $$$

Price guide for a two-course meal for two, with a glass of wine each where alcohol is available:

$$$$$ over Dhs500
$$$$ Dhs400–500
$$$ Dhs200–400
$$ Dhs100–200
$ below Dhs100

Another popular Lebanese eatery that's known for the generous size of its special set-menu options on Thursday evenings. Shisha is available, and belly dancing displays are put on here, too. Alcohol. Dress: smart casual.

Automatic

Al Riqqa Road, Deira, also on Jumeira Road, and Sheikh Zayed Road; tel: 04 227 7824; daily 9am–1am; $–$$

An informal Lebanese restaurant with pavement seating on an attractive avenue that offers fine mezze served with fresh vegetables. There's a branch of the same establishment at The Beach Centre in Jumeira (tel: 04 349 4888). Both outlets are usually filled with diners enjoying the unpretentious food, generous portions and generally excellent value for money dining experience. No alcohol. Dress: casual.

Beachcombers

Jumeirah Beach Hotel, Jumeira; tel: 04 348 0000; www.jumeirahbeach hotel.com/dining; daily 7.30am– midnight; $$$

This Southeast Asian restaurant with a thatched terrace overlooking the spectacular Burj Al Arab is difficult to beat for its views. There's an à-la-carte menu for lunch and buffet for dinner. Families are welcome. Alcohol. Dress: smart casual.

Chhappan Bhog

Sheikh Khalifa Bin Zayed/Trade Centre Road, Bur Dubai; tel: 04 396 8176; daily 12.30–2.30pm and 8–11.30pm; $–$$

Above from far left: alfresco dining at Beachcombers; Gordon Ramsay's stylish Verre.

The North Indian vegetarian meals served here are so delicious that they will appeal to the taste buds of even the most die-hard meat eater. No alcohol. Dress: casual.

Marina Seafood Restaurant

Jumeirah Beach Hotel, Jumeira Road; tel: 04 348 0000; www. jumeirahbeachhotel/dining; daily noon–3pm and 6pm–1am; $$$$$

The setting – right by the Burj Al Arab, on an island linked by a narrow causeway to the Jumeirah Beach Hotel, accessible by golf cart – is pure James Bond fantasy. The open-air bar above the restaurant offers excellent 360-degree views. Alcohol. Dress: smart.

Pierchic

Al Qasr Hotel, Madinat Jumeirah; tel: 04 366 6730; www.madinat jumeirah.com; daily noon–3pm and 7–11.30pm; $$$$$

A fabulous seafood restaurant at the end of its own wooden pier with stun-

Right: Pierchic.

ning views of Burj Al Arab and the Madinat Jumeirah resort. Probably the most romantic restaurant in Dubai. Alcohol. Dress: smart.

Sho Cho

Dubai Marine Beach Resort, Jumeira; tel: 04 346 1111; www.dxbmarine.com; daily 7pm–2.30am; $$$

This stylish hang-out for Dubai's beautiful people overlooks a small beach and is part sushi restaurant and part cocktail bar and DJ club. Alcohol. Dress: smart casual.

Spectrum On One

The Fairmont Dubai, Sheikh Zayed Road; tel: 04 311 8101; daily 7pm–1am; $$$$

This contemporary European restaurant in a hip hotel across the highway from the exhibition centre is consistently rated as one of Dubai's best. Alcohol. Dress: smart casual.

Tagine

One&Only Royal Mirage Hotel, Al Mina Al Siyahi; tel: 04 399 9999; Tue–Sun 7–11.30pm; $$$

Expect excellent Moroccan food, live music and a wonderful atmosphere (recalling a bygone, pre-oil age) at Tagine, set in one of Dubai's leading hotels. It is also conveniently located next to the fashionable Kasbar nightclub. Alcohol. Dress: smart casual.

Trader Vic's

Crowne Plaza, Sheikh Zayed Road and Souk Madinat Jumeirah; tel: 04 331 1111; www.tradervics.com; daily noon–3pm and 7pm–2.30am; $$$$

A happy mishmash of styles – Polynesia meets Asia and the Caribbean – this lively bar and restaurant has live music and a party atmosphere. Alcohol. Dress: smart casual.

Vu's

Emirates Towers Hotel, Sheikh Zayed Road; tel: 04 330 0000; www.jumeirah.com; daily 12.30–3pm and 7.30–11.30pm; $$$$$

As the name suggests, Vu's not only offers fine dining but also stunning views from the 50th floor of the landmark Emirates Towers hotel. This is reputedly the highest restaurant in the Middle East – at least until Burj Dubai is complete. Alcohol. Dress: smart.

Zheng He's

Mina A'Salam, Madinat Jumeirah; tel: 04 366 8888; www.madinat jumeirah.com; daily noon–3pm and 7–11.30pm; $$$$

Regarded as one of the top Chinese restaurants in Dubai, Zheng He's' sumptuous hotel setting takes some beating. Alcohol. Dress: smart casual.

Price guide for a two-course meal for two, with a glass of wine each where alcohol is available:

$$$$$	over Dhs500
$$$$	Dhs400–500
$$$	Dhs200–400
$$	Dhs100–200
$	below Dhs100

Snacking

For a traditional snack between meals try a *manouchet zaatar*, Arabic bread with thyme, sesame seeds and olive oil, or *manouchet jebneh*, Arabic bread with cheese. These are best eaten straight from the oven at one of the numerous Lebanese bakeries in the city.

OVER 250 DESTINATIONS
IN 14 LANGUAGES

Let us be your guide

Your first visit – or a familiar destination? A short stay – or an extended exploration? Whatever your needs, there's an Insight Guide in a format to suit you. From Alaska to Zanzibar, we'll help you discover your world with great pictures, insightful text, easy-to-use maps, and invaluable advice.

www.insightguides.com

INSIGHT GUIDES

CREDITS

Insight Step by Step Dubai
Written by: Matt Jones
Series Editor: Clare Peel
Cartography Editors: James Macdonald, Zoë Goodwin
Picture Manager: Steve Lawrence
Art Editor: Ian Spick
Production: Kenneth Chan

Photography by: Apa: Matt Jones except:
4 Corners 24–5, 49B; Abu Dhabi Tourism 90B, 90M, 90MT, 90TR, 91TL, 91TR, 92B, 92TL, 92TR, 93B, 93M, 93TL; Aerogulf 60, 61B; Alamy 35T, 68T, 69T, 71T, 78-79, 80T, 84B, 85T, 88T; Camerapix 86CTL; Corbis 8–9, 11B, 11TR, 23T, 68T, 70T; Dubai Tourist Board 11TL, 12TL, 14TL, 42TL; Getty 2–3, 16TL, 34T, 36T, 47B, 50B, 64T, 65T, 94–5; istockphoto 2BL, 2BM, 2BR, 2ML, 2MM, 2MR, 10TR, 12B, 12TR, 13TL, 16TR, 24ML, 61T, 66B, 66T, 77T, 78TR, 79TR, 84T, 87T, 98, 99, 108B; 22T TopFoto.
Front cover: main image: Corbis; bottom left: superstock; bottom right: istockphoto.

Printed by: Insight Print Services (Pte) Ltd, 38 Joo Koon Road, Singapore 628990

© 2008 Apa Publications GmbH & Co. Verlag KG (Singapore branch)

First Edition 2008

CONTACTING THE EDITORS

We would appreciate it if readers would alert us to errors or outdated information by writing to us at insight@apaguide.co.uk or Apa Publications, PO Box 7910, London SE1 1WE, UK.

www.insightguides.com

DISTRIBUTION

WORLDWIDE

**Apa Publications GmbH & Co. Verlag KG
(Singapore branch)**
38 Joo Koon Road
Singapore 628990
Tel: (65) 6865 1600
Fax: (65) 6861 6438

UK AND IRELAND

GeoCenter International Ltd
Meridian House, Churchill Way West
Basingstoke, Hampshire, RG21 6YR
Tel: (44) 01256 817 987
Fax: (44) 01256 817 988

UNITED STATES

Langenscheidt Publishers, Inc.
36–36 33rd Street, 4th Floor
Long Island City, NY 11106
Tel: (1) 718 784 0055
Fax: (1) 718 784 0640

AUSTRALIA

Universal Publishers
1 Waterloo Road
Macquarie Park
NSW 2113
Tel: (61) 2 9857 3700
Fax: (61) 2 9888 9074

NEW ZEALAND

Hema Maps New Zealand Ltd (HNZ)
Unit D, 24 Ra ORA Drive
East Tamaki, Auckland
Tel: (64) 9 273 6459
Fax: (64) 9 273 6479

INDEX

Pangkor Laut Resort, Malaysia

OVER 250 DESTINATIONS IN 14 LANGUAGES

Let us be your guide

Your first visit – or a familiar destination? A short stay – or an extended exploration? Whatever your needs, there's an Insight Guide in a format to suit you. From Alaska to Zanzibar, we'll help you discover your world with great pictures, insightful text, easy-to-use maps, and invaluable advice.